RETURN TO TUSCANY

RETURN TO TUSCANY

RECIPES FROM A TUSCAN COOKERY SCHOOL

Giancarlo and Katie Caldesi

contents

Returning to Tuscany

As the final wooden spoon and measuring jug were squeezed into the boot of our car, Giancarlo looked at me and said, 'Enough, we have to go'. The stress of trying to finish everything at work, packing, persuading two children to leave their home and apprehension about what was in store for us made us bicker like children for the first couple of hours of our journey to Tuscany. We had decided to open a cookery school there for September 2005, and we were going to be filmed doing it.

We knew it was going to be hard work with new students arriving and old ones departing on the same day and that most of the time we would be 'miked up' and followed by cameras.

When we reached Dover, late at night in the pouring rain, we carried the sleeping children into a cheap hotel next to a noisy bus station and tried to sleep. The next day the sun shone and we got up early for the ferry to France. The children were excited and so were we. Over the next three days, Giancarlo and I had time to calm down. As the landscape grew more beautiful around us, our stress disappeared and we talked over every aspect of what we expected of the next few weeks.

We had been married in Montepulciano, Tuscany, in June, opened our cookery school in London in July, honeymooned in the Caribbean in August and now we had packed up to run a cookery school in Italy for a few weeks in September. Friends and family told us we were crazy and they were probably right! In fact, the school in London should have opened in April, giving us more time to see it established before we abandoned it. As it was, we had to brief the staff of our restaurants and new cooking school and leave the businesses in their hands.

Giancarlo's father, Memmo, had died in Tuscany in the summer of 2004. This personal loss was compounded by the tragic sale of the home that had been in the family for generations. We knew this would be an emotional journey for Giancarlo; he wanted to have a memorial service for his father and sort out the last of his belongings. He feared he was losing touch with his roots, so we were keen to re-establish a foothold in Tuscany.

Before committing to buying a house in Tuscany, we thought we'd see how we felt about living there either temporarily or permanently; what the children would think of it; how they would settle into Italian school life; and what we'd think about living in the countryside instead of central London. We also liked the idea of bringing people to Tuscany and teaching them to cook – so the idea of setting up a Tuscan cookery school was born.

In December 2004 we had looked at several villas to rent for the following summer and then come across Hotel Le Rotelle (right) outside the small town of Torrita di Siena. It was in a beautiful rural location near Montepulciano, where Giancarlo had grown up. It had a wonderful view, a large newly built pool and, despite being a hotel, the building seemed small enough to still feel homely. The only trouble was that there was no one there when we went to visit. We peered in through the windows and could just about make out the kitchen, the restaurant and one of the bedrooms. We fell in love with it and then had to rush to catch the plane home. Over Christmas we negotiated a deal with the owners and started advertising the cookery school. On our next visit, in February, we checked out the inside and decided to have our wedding reception there.

That way we could spend a week ironing out any problems before opening the school.

Ironically, it was the loss of his father and his family home that led Giancarlo to realize that this was the right time to return to Tuscany, to rediscover his roots, his family and the local recipes – an opportunity to reconnect with his culture and to introduce me to his past. We had been living together for eight years and now we wanted to get married. Giancarlo wanted to have a big wedding, to invite both English and Italian families, and to have a chance to get to know his vast array of cousins, both close and distant, all over again.

Why Giancarlo left Tuscany

Giancarlo and his family had endured poverty for many years, as did many Italians at the time of his childhood. This, coupled with visits from a wealthy cousin who had emigrated to America, gave him a wanderlust, a need to discover the world, abandon his farming background and search for a more prosperous way of life. Until he was 17 years old he had never set foot out of Tuscany and his family had never taken holidays. At the earliest opportunity Giancarlo left home to work as a *commis* waiter in nearby Chianciano Terme. He was only 13 years old, worked all hours of the day, took no breaks and lived in. Although his wages were very low and he wasn't treated well, it was far away from farm life and the hardships of living off the land.

His next move was to a completely different world – the bustling metropolis of Rome. He worked as a waiter at the Hilton Cavalieri and loved it. He had to leave a year later, however, to go into the army. Conscription has only just ended in Italy and Giancarlo, like all his contemporary male friends, had to do his military service. As his work experience was in restaurants, he was given the job of waiter in an officers' mess. However, Giancarlo, ever the daredevil, had different ideas – he wanted to be a paratrooper. He believed this would give him status among his peers, would make him devastatingly attractive to the opposite sex and, above all, provide great excitement – every boy's dream! I think his days as a paratrooper gave him an incredible inner strength. He never gives up and works long hours without a break – he also expects others to do the same and cannot bear laziness or lack of punctuality. He never wears a watch but is always on time whereas I always wear one but am always 10 minutes late. It drives him mad!

After his two years' army service Giancarlo was able to continue working at the Hilton Cavlieri. This time he asked for a transfer abroad and the first vacancy that came up was in London. After a spell at the Park Lane Hilton and several other restaurants he settled for some years at the City Circle, a popular restaurant in the heart of the City of London. It was boom time and he enjoyed a good salary and saw the kind of wealth he had never seen in Tuscany.

He soon developed the ambition to have his own place and the opportunity arose when he was working for a restaurant group that went bust. He bought one of its restaurants with two friends and the partners ran Portico in the City for a few years. This allowed them to buy another restaurant. It was there that Giancarlo lost his temper with a chef, asked him to leave immediately and donned his apron. He started to cook from that moment on. The restaurant was a huge success and this enabled him to set up the Caldesi restaurant in Marylebone Lane, which we still have. Giancarlo started it 14 years ago and four years later I arrived on the scene to give it a facelift. I've been there ever since.

How it all started …

I was a painter of walls, a muralist, and living in Eastbourne when a commission arose through a mutual friend who asked me to come and help him paint a cellar bar in London. I promptly packed my portfolio and went off to meet Mr Caldesi who had, in fact, donned an old pair of tight blue overalls and decided to clean the stairs that day. On arrival at the bar I walked past the odd-looking man scrubbing furiously on the stairs, who had to move out of my way to let me past. When I got inside I asked where I could meet Mr Caldesi, and his partner took great delight in telling me I had just pushed him out of the way and knocked him off the stairs as I descended them!

Giancarlo tells me he knew we would be together from that first instant. It took me a little longer to know he was the man for me – the overalls really weren't that flattering! However, it wasn't long before the suave man who usually dressed in beautiful Italian suits and reeked of expensive aftershave grew on me. Our mutual love of food, art and each other grew rapidly. We are now married and have two children, Giorgio, nearly six, and Flavio, four (right). They too enjoy food and love to cook, which is fortunate as I don't excel at playing trains and cars!

It was a year or so before Giancarlo took me to Tuscany to meet his family and show me his region of Italy. His parents had been *contadini* or peasant farmers, and had a smallholding in a rural area. The house had been in his family for generations, and his father showed me where they had kept cows, pigs and rabbits and we collected eggs from the few remaining chickens. He still kept a fully stocked herb garden and every day he picked basil and rosemary for his cooking. When Giancarlo was a boy his parents were almost totally self-sufficient, but more recently

the crops and animals had gone. His family had known great poverty, as had most Italians after the Second World War but, although he has no memories of childhood luxuries, Giancarlo does have very fond memories of wonderful food and wine, of parties and celebrations.

His parents have now gone but his remaining family and friends have warmly welcomed both me and our children. Nello Ceccuzzi, Giancarlo's childhood neighbour, is in many respects a second brother to him, and his wife Livia and their son Daniele have become an intrinsic part of my life. We have shared tears, happiness and always good food. This generous, loyal family have a smallholding and are 80 per cent self-sufficient – Nello tends to the orchard, Daniele looks after the vines and Livia is a wonderful cook. It is from

them that Giancarlo and I have learnt the most. The Ceccuzzi family are *contadini* and Nello (above left, with Daniele) delighted in telling two of the film crew that, as they were from the town, they wouldn't be able to understand how the wine-making machines worked – only *contadini* would be able to work it out!

Italians are fiercely proud of their origins. Whenever two of them meet abroad the first thing they ask is, 'Where are you from?' – often followed by, 'Who do you support?' Without exception, every Italian believes passionately that their region is the best, their football team, their food, their spaghetti *ragu* recipe – everything. After all, the unification of the 20 regions as one country only happened in 1870.

Tuscan food: rooted in tradition

'What strange people the Italians are,' I hear myself say as I travel around Italy. On the one hand, they are so modern and they encourage

weird and wonderful ground-breaking design in fashion, furniture, lighting and architecture – yet, on the other hand, they are firmly rooted in their traditions. And this is what is so fascinating about their food. The average Italian knows how to make a *ragu* and the recipe will have come from one of his or her grandmothers, and that is how the family always makes it. The recipe won't have changed in the last hundred years or so and nor will it in the hands of the next generation. Italians would never consider it. You can ask a Tuscan, 'Why don't you have salt in your bread? Don't you think it would taste better?' 'Yes,' he or she will say, 'but that's how it is done in Tuscany. Saltless bread, it's always been like that and it always will be.' I frequently find Italian's spectacularly closed minds infuriating, but I have to admit their food is delicious. If it works, why change it? Lasagne has been pleasing people since the Renaissance. So who am I to introduce a twist to this classic dish?

Giancarlo's recipes are by and large those of his mother and grandmother. There are some I have been brave enough to add to, but only after they have been tested and approved by Giancarlo, his family and his friends.

Giancarlo and I both wanted to see the Tuscans cook their food in their own country. I'd been visiting Tuscany for seven years but still hadn't spent long in anyone's kitchen. Giancarlo wanted to work with his own people again and learn from them. Even within Tuscany the food varies from the coastal regions to the inland area. Montepulciano in southern Tuscany, where Giancarlo comes from, is a long way from the coast – a land of hills and lakes, of verdant plains and rugged forests. But times had changed since Giancarlo lived there, with fish being more easily available, even away from the coast, bigger and better markets and many more restaurants.

Artisan foods are well respected and we discovered fantastic supplies of Cinta Senese pork, *chianina* beef, pecorino cheeses and many, many more delicious products, all made by enthusiastic, passionate people. Even the younger generation are keen to make the most of their own produce wherever possible, making their own wines and olive oil, and tending their own fruit trees. By shopping locally at farm shops and markets we were able to buy an enormous amount of good-quality fruit and vegetables at very reasonable prices. After one of our trips to buy food, we fed 11 people for just 55 Euros (about £38).

Italians tend only to eat foods that are in season – there is usually little available out of season and what there is, is generally tasteless or foreign! You never see Tuscans buying tomatoes in December because they will eat their own bottled ones.

Tuscan food has two clear origins: rich and poor. *La cucina nobile* is from the nobility and uses expensive cuts of meat and exotic spices. It dates back to the Renaissance and beyond, even to Roman times. In the Renaissance, Tuscany was influenced by the spice trade and, to show off their wealth, cooks used spices such as cinnamon, cardamom and ginger. *La cucina povera* comes from the *contadini* and is peasant cooking at its best. As necessity is the mother of all invention, so Tuscan mothers are the inventors of an amazing array of recipes that require only local ingredients. How many dishes can you invent to use up stale bread and beans? Ask me and I will tell you if you have a few days to spare!

Our students on the cookery course were surprised by the amount of salt and olive oil used in Tuscan cooking. You cannot expect to re-create any of the dishes you'll find in the following pages if you are not prepared to be generous with these. The same goes for herbs – they should be fresh and preferably picked from your window box or garden, or bought from your local supermarket. Tuscans rarely use dried herbs, apart from oregano, which is not widely available in Tuscany.

I have discovered so much about Tuscan food as a result of running the cookery school and being able to spend so much time with Giancarlo's circle of family and friends, as well as the staff in the hotel in Tuscany: Giancarlo the *fungaiolo* (mushroom-hunter), Stefano our pastry chef, Gregorio our head chef and Aunt Gina, who shared her cake recipes with me.

Lifestyle and attitudes to food

Italians know their food. And they talk about it all the time. For some this might be irritating – for me, it's fascinating and makes me feel at ease – aah, people after my own heart!

In particular, Italians are passionate about food from their region. They may not be great cooks themselves but their mothers, or at least

RECIPE FOR A WEEK
WITH GIANCARLO AND KATIE

by Janet Appleton, WEEK 3, SEPTEMBER 2005

1 student
1 small measure of enthusiasm
1 week of holiday, well planned
some well-earned Euros
1 easy journey
1 large pinch of encouragement from
  family and friends
1 measure of curiosity, well seasoned
  with concentration

Mix everything together well, in Tuscan sunshine. Allow to rise. Garnish as necessary for presentation. Serve to friends with Italian wines, plenty of time and lots of conversation. Enjoy!

their grandmothers, probably were. Most will have basic cooking skills and be able to rustle up a few pasta sauces from scratch without having to resort to jars. They will have been brought up eating smaller portions of grown-up food instead of food designed for children, such as reconstituted fish in the shape of a dinosaur or yoghurts laden with sugar and colouring. The menu at Giorgio and Flavio's nursery in Tuscany read like the menu at our restaurant. Fresh stuffed ravioli for starters, followed by sea bass with green beans in tomato sauce. I could have easily stayed there just for the food!

Italian families still eat together more than the average British family. When they go out to eat, children go too. This exposure to good food and restaurants at a young age, at school and at home, means young adults are likely to go out to eat rather than just to drink. They'll go clubbing, and they're not perfect when it comes to drugs and alcohol, but they certainly know about good food. When Italians settle down and start families they are expected to cook good food at home for friends and, of course, use every opportunity to go out to eat and socialize.

Breakfast is a social visit to a bar for a coffee and croissant. Lunch is a long break of at least an hour and a half so that food can be enjoyed – many people go home to eat and sleep. Then it's back to work from 3pm until 7pm before dinner with family or friends.

The importance given to eating in Italy breeds a culture of caring for food in all its aspects – the selling, buying and cooking of it as well as its consumption. Meals are to be savoured and enjoyed. Everything stops for food, and long may that last. The Slow Food organization, a movement against the effects of fast food, started in Italy. For more information, visit www.slowfood.com.

Our school in London

We loved our life at the Caldesi restaurant. We lived 'above the shop' for several years and always ate the food cooked in the restaurant. We raised Giorgio there for two years and moved out when Flavio was four days old (he came early!). In 2002 we opened Caffé Caldesi as a sister restaurant to the Caldesi restaurant, combining a formal à la carte restaurant upstairs, serving food from all the regions of Italy, with an Italian-style café/bar downstairs for coffees and light lunches.

During our time at the Caldesi restaurant we began teaching groups of regular customers who had expressed an interest in learning more about food. This developed into more formal lessons on Tuscan cooking, which was Giancarlo's speciality, and demand grew for our courses. People enjoyed our scheduled classes but also asked for tailor-made cooking days or nights – to celebrate a birthday, for instance. We also got anything from office groups on a team-building day to hen parties – two hours of cooking followed by lunch or dinner eating what has been cooked. This meant we were running out of space teaching in the two restaurant kitchens so we decided to start our school. La Cucina Caldesi opened its kitchen doors in July 2005.

Our school in Tuscany

Giancarlo and I wanted our course on Tuscan cooking to be accessible to anyone, whether they were experienced cooks or not. And indeed the students who came to the school all had different reasons for attending, whether it was learning to cook for the first time, finding new ideas for family meals or honing skills to open their own restaurant. Since we taught only small groups of students, over four days or a week, there was time to see to people's individual needs or interests.

We structured the course in Tuscany around different aspects of Tuscan cooking, and taught each one on a different day.

On Saturday, students enjoyed a typical Tuscan dinner, which we prepared for them. On Sunday they got up early and learnt to cook a Sunday lunch, concentrating on meat or poultry. Monday was antipasti day and started with a trip to the market to buy food for a selection of light dishes for lunch. Tuesday was for pasta-making, followed by preserving tomatoes and making jam at Livia's house. Wednesday there was a wine-tasting trip to Castello Banfi, an Italian castle and winery, followed by dinner at its restaurant. Thursday was a well-deserved day off to explore or shop, followed by cocktails and dinner *al fresco*. Friday was for fish – after a trip to the fish shop in Siena the students cooked local perch for lunch. In the evening it was their turn to cook dinner for us. It was good for them to prepare the dishes we had taught them while we were still together as it meant they could catch up on anything they had missed. Throughout the week we taught how to make bread and desserts as well.

The chapters in this book reflect the course; each one starts with a lesson on one aspect of Tuscan cookery, followed by the recipes we taught in Italy. We have also added a few from our restaurants, several personal favourites and some from our London courses, which we wanted to share.

Tuscany is an inspiration to us still – the lifestyle, the generosity of the people and the beauty of the countryside. I urge you to travel there and experience it for yourself. We loved being there and it answered many questions for us. Yes, we do want to buy a house and carry on teaching there. For 2006, however, we are looking forward to going back to Hotel Le Rotelle for the month of July, to run the school again.

antipasti

AND VEGETABLES

salted sardines with chopped red onion • white winter salad with honey dressing • tomato bruschetta • bresaola, rocket and parmesan rolls • balsamic onions • gregorio's aubergine slices • stuffed chillies • oven-roasted vegetables with crumbled goats' cheese, thyme and parsley • black crostini • mushroom crostini • sformato of carrots • porcini and pecorino refried mash • cannellini bean and rosemary mash • luciano's roast potatoes • green beans in tomato sauce

antipasti and vegetables

Antipasti literally means 'before the meal', and is a selection of local produce served on a large platter if people are sharing or on smaller plates for individual portions. The first time I enjoyed a traditional antipasti platter was in the heart of Tuscany, in the hill-top town of Montalcino. The venue was a dimly lit enoteca, an Italian wine bar, in a castle. I was served a wooden platter of pecorino cheeses and locally produced wafer-thin prosciutto with a huge balloon glass of Brunello, the hearty red wine of the region. I was won over.

It seemed the best way to enjoy the rich flavours of Tuscany – simply and deliciously without complicated sauces and fussy presentation. In fact I was so inspired that the design of Caffè Caldesi, our *enoteca* in London, is based on the original in Montalcino and our antipasti platter to share is one of our bestsellers.

Since then I have discovered many other antipasti dishes, from vegetables *sott' olio* (chargrilled vegetables preserved in oil with garlic and herbs) to crostini (toasted bread with a variety of toppings) and imported tiny Calabrian peppers stuffed with anchovies, capers and tuna. The choice is endless but the staples are nearly always the same: dried or cured meats and cheese. In the restaurants of Pienza, another of Tuscany's beautiful, ancient fortified towns, which is famous for its pecorino, they serve different varieties and maturities of the cheese with either honey, mustard, fruits or plum jam.

Create your own antipasti platter by arranging a selection of your favourite produce on a wooden chopping board. The children frequently have this for breakfast or lunch. They share (in a way!) halved cherry tomatoes, cucumber, salami, cured sausages, *bresaola*, cheeses and fruit cut up into small pieces that are easy to pick at.

Crostini: toasts and toppings

Whether dining in a restaurant or at home, Tuscans usually expect crostini to be served with the antipasti. These are toasted slices of bread with various toppings and they might include *crostini neri* (Black Crostini, page 32) made with slow-cooked chicken livers, capers and a fortified wine, *crostini porcini e salsicce* topped with porcini and crumbled sausage, or *crostini radicchio e pecorino* with shredded radicchio and pecorino.

Tomatoes: a basic ingredient

One of the most widely used ingredients in Italian cookery, tomatoes come in a huge variety of shapes and sizes. Large, round green varieties, or long, slim green-and-red ones, are nearly always used for salad or for making into a green tomato jam. *Pomodori cuore di bue*, which are the shape of an ox heart, are also good for salads. Plum-shaped San Marzano are popular for cooking and reducing to make a richly flavoured sauce. They are also perfect for preserving in bottles. Cherry tomatoes are often sold on the vine and are usually eaten fresh or semi-dried.

Bunches of tomatoes – *pomodori di menza* are the usual round ones – are hung in a ventilated place to dry from the end of the season in August until around Christmas. Tuscans dry tomatoes in their garages – strings of them hang above the vehicles. The contrast of old traditions alongside new cars always makes me smile.

Semi-dried tomatoes are squashed on a piece of bread, topped with olive oil, salt and basil and eaten as *bruschetta al pomodoro*. This version of bruschetta has a richer flavour than the classic recipe made with fresh tomatoes (page 24). The Italian name for tomatoes comes from the first ones eaten in Europe, which were yellow, hence *pomo d'oro* (golden apple).

Pecorino and other cheeses

Each cheese and meat stall at a market has a wide selection of pecorino, the sheeps' cheese made originally in Sardinia and now also in Tuscany. The reason for this is that when the feudal system of peasant farming collapsed in

the 1960s, the local people went to the towns to find work. This opened up opportunities for Sardinian families to come to Tuscany bringing with them their traditions, including their skills as shepherds and producers of pecorino. At the market Giancarlo and I met a lady selling cheese who was obviously of Sardinian descent as she had blue-black hair and big dark eyes. She told me her grandfather had come to Tuscany and that her family followed his cheese-making methods. They liked to preserve their cheeses in ash, walnut leaves or straw to impart different flavours.

There are three main types of pecorino: *fresco* (up to three months old); *semi-stagionato* (over three months old); and *stagionato* (over six months old). Many producers keep cheeses in their cellars for several years as great delicacies.

Other popular cheeses include mozzarella, *burrata* (a young, creamy mozzarella), Gorgonzola and sometimes goats' cheese. When buying hard cheeses such as pecorino,

don't store them in the fridge, but in a cool place. It is at room temperature that their flavour can be fully appreciated.

Salads, vegetables and fruits

Salads are not generally served as side dishes in southern Tuscany. The locals prefer to eat pasta, meat and salad in that order. At first glance, the salads are usually not very exciting, although the leaves have more flavour than their UK counterparts – the pepperiness of the rocket leaves will blow your socks off! But scratch under the surface of the average Tuscan diet and you will find a huge array of salads and vegetable dishes. The further south you go in Italy it seems, the wider the variety of vegetables and the more they are eaten. So we decided to bring a few recipes north, including Gregorio's Aubergine Slices (page 28).

Fruit and vegetables are sold according to the season. We spent a summer and autumn in Tuscany enjoying plums, figs, melons and peaches, and Sicilian unwaxed lemons with the leaves on to show their freshness. Italians simply don't eat fresh fruit and vegetables out of season because almost nothing is imported. They are proud to tell you where their food is grown and enjoy different produce throughout the year. With the preserving techniques they have inherited Tuscans can enjoy fruit preserved in syrup or liqueurs, and a variety of jams and pickled vegetables, in winter.

Mushrooms: an autumn delicacy

Mushroom-hunting is a national pastime in Italy and a popular day out. When we went mushroom-picking in autumn with our students we found fresh porcini and chanterelles. Packets of dried porcini are sold all year round, but nothing beats the feeling of finding your first fresh one. Giancarlo, the *fungaiolo* who took me mushroom-hunting, said you have to be a good liar to be a good mushroom-hunter. That's because if people ask you where you found your mushrooms you have to lie about it in case they go there too! Giancarlo's love of his native Siena was obvious – he taught me the Sienese word for each mushroom we found and pointed out the ones that were edible but that he didn't think were worth picking. He referred to them as *capra* (goat) and said only the Florentines would eat them. I asked why he despised the Florentines so much and he told me of the war between Siena and Florence. Even though I reminded him it had ended a few centuries ago, he still bore a grudge! (For information on mushroom-finding trips in the UK try www.fungitobewith.)

Salumi: a variety of cold meats

Salumi is the generic word for all types of dried or cured meat, including salami and those mysterious brown paper packages tied up with string that you see hanging up in Italian delis.

Looking at the counter in a delicatessen or into a meat van at a market, it is hard not to be impressed by the range of different types of dried and cured meat, nearly always made on local farms and each one unique. In Tuscany, the two types of *salumi* that stand out are *finocchiona*, a salami flavoured with fennel seeds, and *cinghiale* or wild boar salami. The brown paper packages tied up with string contain *lombo*, a cured loin of pork, which comes in different stages of maturity. Often a few are cut in half so that customers can see the extent of the curing process. The dark edges show how many months old a *lombo* is. A really old one will be dark in colour with a strong flavour and a young one will be still pink with a subtle taste.

The strings of cured sausages suspended on hooks are either pork or wild boar. They can be sliced and eaten as antipasti or used in a pasta sauce. A good deli will also have a huge roll of mortadella, sometimes up to 30 cm (12 in) in diameter. This is made from finely ground sausagemeat studded with pistachios or olives. We also usually buy *bresaola*, a cured beef alternative to prosciutto, which is very rich in iron.

The most sought after *salumi* comes from the Cinta Senese pig (above), which provides sausages, *sopressata* (a type of salami), *rigatino* (streaky bacon), *lombo* (loin), *fiore di spalla* (shoulder) and prosciutto. It also has a wide band of fat on its belly, which is highly prized as a source of *lardo* (white fat that is eaten in thin slices). This beautiful black pig, with a belt of white around its middle, was nearly extinct for the simple reason that the more common white pig was more commercial, as it was reared more easily and less problematic to keep. In Tuscany I visited two farms where only Cinta Senese were

reared, and the passion of the farmers and the effort they put in to their work is extraordinary.

Fish for antipasti

Preserved fish for antipasti are easily available in delis or at market stalls. However, the choice is usually limited to sardines, anchovies, tuna, cured eels and mackerel.

Olives and vegetables sott' olio

Olives and vegetables preserved in oil provide a splash of colour and plenty of flavour in any antipasti selection. There are three main varieties of olive, each tasty in a different way. Small dark ones are good for cooking and can be eaten on their own. Large green olives are also often eaten straight, and are used for stuffing and deep frying. Mixed olives are a good choice to serve with aperitifs.

Sun-dried tomatoes, capers in salt and peppers and aubergines *sott' olio* (in oil) are sold in jars at markets, usually by the vendors who sell cheese.

If you are lucky enough to find small sardines preserved in salt in an Italian deli you will have a simple antipasto at your fingertips. If you can't find sardines, try buying tins or jars of anchovies packed in salt at your local delicatessen or supermarket and use them in the same way. Don't worry about the finished dish tasting too salty. If you wash the sardines or anchovies well before you start, you'll find the sweetness of the red onions cuts through any residual saltiness.

salted sardines with chopped red onion

SERVES 4 AS A STARTER

16 salted sardines or salted
  anchovies
1 small red onion, finely chopped
2 sprigs fresh parsley, roughly torn
extra-virgin olive oil, for drizzling

TO SERVE
white crusty farmhouse bread

Rinse the sardines thoroughly under cold running water to remove the salt. Using a sharp knife, make a slit down the belly of the fish and pull the spine out with your fingers. If using anchovies, simply rinse them.

Dry the fish on kitchen paper on both sides and arrange them on a serving platter.

Sprinkle the onion and parsley over the fish and drizzle with olive oil. Serve with white crusty farmhouse bread.

Tuscany has such a wide variety of honeys. Inspired by a wonderful traditional honey festival we went to in Montalcino, I invented this dish with two of our students, Ruth Joseph and Helen Riglia. We made it with the first walnuts that dropped from the tree in Livia's garden. For this winter version, I simply use pine nuts or blanched almonds instead of walnuts. If you can't find pecorino, use fresh Parmesan instead of the mature pecorino and mature Cheddar instead of the young pecorino. Most combinations of cheeses would work, but you need one strong, hard one and one softer one.

white winter salad with honey dressing

SERVES 4

FOR THE SALAD
2 ripe, firm pears
2 apples
2 celery sticks
100 g (4 oz) mature pecorino
100 g (4 oz) young pecorino
30 g (1½ oz) pine nuts
pomegranate seeds, to garnish

FOR THE DRESSING
2 tablespoons honey
2 tablespoons extra-virgin olive oil
1–2 tablespoons honey vinegar or
  lemon juice
salt and freshly ground black
  pepper

Cut the pears, apples, celery, mature pecorino and young pecorino into slices or cubes, as you prefer.

Lightly toast the pine nuts in a dry frying pan for 2–3 minutes, taking care that they don't burn.

Mix all the ingredients for the dressing together in a large bowl. Add the prepared salad ingredients and mix well.

Transfer the salad to a serving dish, garnish with pomegranate seeds and serve straight away.

There are three recipes here – tomato salsa, Tuscan garlic bread and the combination of the two: tomato bruschetta. This is a popular dish in the UK, and still a staple on restaurant menus in Italy. There is nothing better than late summer's sweet tomatoes with extra-virgin olive oil and basil. Our friend Nello, who grows five types of tomato, showed us how to make his version when we were in Tuscany, and Gino Borella, who used to be head chef at San Lorenzo in Knightsbridge, gave us the tip of first draining the tomatoes, so that they can be prepared a little in advance and placed on the bread just before serving.

tomato bruschetta

MAKES 10 SLICES

FOR THE FRESH TOMATO SALSA
10 very ripe tomatoes or
   30 cherry tomatoes
handful of fresh basil leaves,
   torn into small pieces, plus
   extra to garnish
salt

FOR THE TUSCAN GARLIC BREAD
1 white farmhouse unsliced loaf
   (slightly stale bread is best)
1 garlic clove
extra-virgin olive oil, for drizzling

Cut the tomatoes into 1 cm ($^1/_2$ in) dice. Mix in a bowl with the basil and a pinch of salt. Pour into a sieve, place over another bowl and leave to drain for 30 minutes to 1 hour.

Cut the loaf into 2 cm ($^3/_4$ in) slices. Toast in a toaster or under a preheated grill (for a really authentic flavour, toast on an open fire).

Rub the garlic over one side only of each slice of toast. Use sparingly for a subtle flavour or generously if you like garlic. Drizzle with plenty of olive oil. Pile the fresh tomato salsa on the bread and drizzle with a little more oil. Garnish with basil and serve.

variation

Nello's version is even simpler. He uses a stale loaf, cut into thick slices, which he rubs on one side with a garlic clove. Then he takes three or four semi-dried cherry tomatoes (which he keeps in his garage hanging on the vine) and squashes them on to the bread. He scatters sea salt and a few torn basil leaves over them, and adds a drizzle of extra-virgin olive oil. This is the way to live!

Bresaola is cured Italian beef. It originated in the Jewish quarter of Rome where it was an alternative to prosciutto, air-dried pork. This recipe is great party food. The rolls are simple to make, can be prepared an hour or two in advance and guests can eat them without the aid of cocktail sticks or forks. Bresaola is a good source of iron so I encourage my children to eat it.

bresaola, rocket and parmesan rolls

SERVES 4

8 slices *bresaola*
handful of rocket leaves, plus extra to garnish
25 g (1 oz) Parmesan or mature pecorino, shaved with a potato peeler
1 lemon, halved (optional)

Spread a slice of *bresaola* open on a chopping board.

Place four or five rocket leaves lengthways on the *bresaola* and top with a Parmesan or pecorino shaving. If desired, squeeze a little lemon juice over the cheese and rocket.

Roll up the *bresaola*. Repeat with the remaining meat, cheese and rocket. Place on a platter and garnish with rocket leaves.

Everyone on the course loved this Italian version of pickled onions. They're really sweet and moreish. We served them as part of a mixed antipasti platter, but they are also great as an accompaniment to meat. The recipe uses two standards of balsamic vinegar, which has been used in Italian cooking since Roman times. Very good balsamic vinegar is aged for years and is therefore expensive. The cheaper, younger variety is fine for cooking the onions, but the recipe does require a little aged vinegar for drizzling over them. If you can't get hold of it, pour 5 tablespoons of the cheaper version into a frying pan, add 1 teaspoon of sugar and reduce for a few minutes to sweeten and thicken the vinegar.

balsamic onions

**SERVES 8–10 AS PART OF A
MIXED ANTIPASTI PLATTER**

16–20 pickling onions, peeled
olive oil, for shallow frying
3 tablespoons balsamic vinegar
  (the cheaper variety), for cooking
aged (more expensive) balsamic
  vinegar, for drizzling

Preheat the oven to 180°C/350°F/Gas 4.

Put the onions and a little olive oil into an ovenproof frying pan and fry gently, for about 3–5 minutes, until golden brown.

Add the cheaper balsamic vinegar. Continue to cook for another 3–5 minutes, tossing the onions frequently until they are well coated and the vinegar has caramelized – it will become thick and sticky.

Transfer the pan to the oven and bake for 10–15 minutes or until the onions are cooked through. (If you don't have an ovenproof frying pan, you can transfer the onions to a small roasting tin.)

Remove the onions from the pan and allow them to cool to room temperature. Drizzle with the aged balsamic vinegar and serve with mixed antipasti.

Gregorio Piazza, our head chef, came to work at Hotel Le Rotelle in Tuscany when we were getting married. He cooked relentlessly for my hungry family, who particularly enjoyed these thinly sliced aubergines, chargilled and then drizzled with oil, mint and garlic. We normally cook them on the chargrill in one of the restaurant kitchens, but at home they could be cooked on a barbecue (see page 82), on a griddle or under the grill.

gregorio's aubergine slices

SERVES 6

100 ml (3¹/₂ fl oz) olive oil
20 g (³/₄ oz) salt
4 aubergines

FOR THE DRESSING
small handful of fresh mint,
  chopped
200 ml (7 fl oz) olive oil
100 ml (3¹/₂ fl oz) balsamic
  vinegar
1 garlic clove, chopped.
1 fresh red chilli, seeded and
  chopped
freshly ground black pepper

Preheat a griddle or the grill until very hot.

Mix the olive oil with the salt. Slice the aubergines lengthways into 5 mm (¹/₄ in) slices. Brush the surface of the aubergine slices on both sides with the oil and salt mixture.

Cook the aubergine slices on both sides on the griddle or under the grill for just a couple of minutes, until brown (with black marks if you are using a griddle).

Meanwhile, prepare the dressing by mixing all the ingredients together.

Allow the aubergine slices to cool to room temperature, then arrange them on a large platter, pour the dressing over and serve.

These little stuffed chillies are usually preserved in oil in jars and sold at markets and delis in Italy. The recipe originated in the south of the country but they are now made everywhere. Be careful when cutting the chillies and don't touch your face or eyes as they will burn. However, after the chillies have been boiled in wine and vinegar, then water, the heat dissipates. In Tuscany, the chillies were small dark-red round ones, called Calabrese. In London, I bought some small, pointed ones, Prairie Fire, from a florist. I checked they were edible and they worked perfectly. Alternatively, look out for the small, sweet red chillies sold in jars in supermarkets – you don't need to cook these ones, just stuff and serve.

stuffed chillies

**MAKES ENOUGH TO FILL
A 300 ML (¹/₂ PINT)
PRESERVING JAR**

18 tiny chillies, tops cut off and
   seeded (you can do this with a
   small spoon)
200 ml (7 fl oz) white wine
400 ml (14 fl oz) white wine
   vinegar
3 salted anchovies
90 g (3¹/₄ oz) tuna in oil, drained
1 tablespoon salted capers, rinsed
1 tablespoon fine breadcrumbs
enough olive oil to cover the
   chillies, if storing

Place the chillies, wine and vinegar in a pan, bring to the boil and boil for 5 minutes. Drain, and discard the cooking liquid. Bring a pan of water to the boil and boil the chillies for 5 minutes. This will get rid of most of their fiery heat. Set aside.

Rinse the anchovies thoroughly under cold running water to remove the salt. Finely chop them with the tuna and capers to form a paste. Combine the paste with the breadcrumbs.

Carefully stuff the chillies with the mixture, filling them right down to the bottom to avoid any air pockets. Do not overfill.

Eat the chillies straight away or place them upright in a jar that has been sterilized by being washed in a dishwasher, or in soapy water for 5 minutes. Cover with olive oil. Push a knife down the sides of the jar, around the chillies, to release any trapped air bubbles, then tap the jar on the table to release more bubbles. Make sure the chillies are completely covered in oil and screw on the lid. They will keep for up to two months in a dark cupboard.

This dish is very popular at Caffé Caldesi. We love eating it at home, too – it's great for entertaining. It's equally delicious made with a mixture of vegetables or just one – the slightly tart cheese balances the crispy sweetness of the roasted vegetables. For a lower-fat choice, or as an accompaniment to a main course dish, omit the cheese. However, always be generous with the olive oil, salt and pepper. The garlic cloves are cooked with their skins on, and do make sure everyone gets one on their plate. The garlic turns to a mild creamy purée inside the skin and can be squeezed out and spread on the vegetables – wonderful!

oven-roasted vegetables
with crumbled goats' cheese, thyme and parsley

SERVES 4

2 red peppers, quartered and
   seeded
1 large aubergine, cut into 1 cm
   (^{1}/$_2$ in) slices
2 medium-sized red onions, cut
   into wedges
4 garlic cloves, unpeeled
few sprigs of fresh thyme
5–6 tablespoons extra-virgin
   olive oil (enough to coat the
   vegetables)
100 g (4 oz) goats' cheese
salt and freshly ground black
   pepper
fresh parsley, torn, to garnish

Preheat the oven to 180°C/350°F/Gas 4.

Place the peppers, aubergine and onions in a roasting tin in a single layer. This is important – more than one layer means the vegetables will steam rather than roast, and become soggy. Squash the garlic cloves lightly with the flat side of a knife to release their flavour. Add to the tin. Scatter the thyme over the vegetables.

Drizzle generously with the olive oil and season with salt and pepper. Make sure all the vegetables are coated with the oil – I usually use my hands to toss the ingredients together.

Roast for 25–35 minutes or until the vegetables are starting to brown around the edges and are cooked through but not soggy.

Transfer to a serving dish and crumble the goats' cheese over them. Garnish with parsley. The vegetables can be left to cool to room temperature before serving, but always add the cheese and parsley at the last minute.

In this staple Tuscan antipasto, the toast is topped with a very dark brown, almost black, soft pâté made from chicken livers. It is delicious as the smooth liver combines so well with the sharpness of the capers and the salt in the anchovies. This is good party food to serve with drinks.

Pane Toscano, the saltless white bread made all over Tuscany, is great for crostini. If you can't get bread without salt, a good white farmhouse loaf will do.

black crostini

SERVES 8

2 tablespoons olive oil
1 red onion, finely chopped
2 garlic cloves, crushed
300 g (11 oz) chicken livers, halved
100 ml (3½ fl oz) Chicken Stock
 (page 44), as necessary
100 ml (3½ fl oz) Marsala or sweet
 sherry
knob of butter
2 anchovies preserved in salt and
 thoroughly rinsed and dried, or
 from a tin
1 dessertspoon capers
16 slices Tuscan or other
 farmhouse-style white bread,
 about 2 cm (¾ in) thick
salt and freshly ground black
 pepper
extra-virgin olive oil, for drizzling
fresh parsley, torn, to garnish
 (optional)

Heat the olive oil in a frying pan and cook the onion and garlic for 8–10 minutes until softened.

Add the livers to the pan, season with salt and pepper and cook over a medium heat for 15–20 minutes until browned all over and soft. Add a ladleful of stock if the liver mixture becomes dry.

Add the Marsala or sherry, and cook for a couple of minutes to reduce. Add the butter and stir well.

Remove the livers, onion and garlic from the pan and place on a chopping board. Roughly chop them with the anchovies and capers. Season again if necessary.

Cut the slices of bread in half or into quarters. Toast the bread on both sides and drizzle with a little extra-virgin olive oil. Spread with the chicken liver pâté. Garnish with a little parsley if you wish (in Italy the crostini are usually served plain). Serve at room temperature on a big platter.

Tuscans are mad on porcini when they come into season in the autumn. As fresh porcini are hard to come by in the UK, try adding 20 g (¾ oz) soaked dried porcini to the wild mushrooms for extra flavour. These crostini are great on their own or with Beef stew (page 88).

mushroom crostini

SERVES 6

4 tablespoons extra-virgin olive oil

small handful of flatleaf parsley leaves, finely chopped

2 medium garlic cloves, peeled and finely chopped

1 fresh red chilli, seeded and finely chopped

2 fresh, medium porcini or 500 g (1 lb 2 oz) wild mushrooms, cleaned and sliced

12 slices Tuscan or other farmhouse-style white bread, about 2 cm (¾ in) thick

salt and freshly ground black pepper

Pour 2 tablespoons of the olive oil into a small bowl, add the parsley, garlic and chilli, and season with salt and pepper.

Remove the stalks from the mushrooms. These can be kept to be chopped and added to a meat dish for a delicate mushroom flavour. Place the mushrooms in another bowl and drizzle the oil mixture over. Toss gently to ensure they are completely covered.

Pour the remaining oil and any remaining oil mixture into a frying pan and place over a low heat. When hot, cook the mushrooms over a low heat for 2 minutes until softened and cooked through. Shake the pan every now and then to turn them.

Cut the slices of bread in half or into quarters. Toast the bread on both sides and drizzle with a little extra-virgin olive oil. Spread with the mushrooms and drizzle over some of the juices from the pan. Serve at room temperature.

This is a Tuscan side dish or contorno. *It is difficult to describe a* sformato *in English and this always trips me up when I come to write menus for the restaurants. It is somewhere between a soufflé, a mash and a purée. This* sformato *has a sweet flavour from the carrots and a light, fluffy texture from the egg whites. It goes beautifully with roast meats.*

sformato of carrots

SERVES 6–8

400 g (14 oz) carrots, chopped
2 egg whites
25 g (1 oz) pecorino or Parmesan, freshly grated

FOR THE BÉCHAMEL SAUCE
30 g (1^1/$_2$ oz) butter, plus an extra knob
25 g (1 oz) plain flour
200 ml (7 fl oz) milk
freshly grated nutmeg, to taste
salt and freshly ground black pepper

Preheat the oven to 200°C/400°F/Gas 6.

Bring a pan of salted water to the boil and cook the carrots until tender.

To make the Béchamel sauce, melt the butter in a small pan, then stir in the flour and cook over a low heat for 1–2 minutes, stirring continuously to make a thick paste. Gradually add the milk, stirring well all the time, then increase the heat and continue to stir until the sauce thickens. Add salt, pepper and nutmeg to taste.

Drain the carrots and mash them finely or process them to make a purée.

Whisk the egg whites until they form very soft peaks.

Stir the sauce and egg whites into the carrots and mix well. Pour into an ovenproof dish and bake for 10 minutes. Dot the top with a little more butter, scatter over the pecorino or Parmesan and bake for a further 10 minutes. The top will form a crust and underneath the carrot will be light and delicious.

porcini and pecorino refried mash

SERVES 4

100 g (4 oz) porcini
1 kg (2¼ lb) potatoes
65 g (2¼ oz) butter
100 g (4 oz) pecorino, freshly grated
175 ml (6 fl oz) milk
4 tablespoons olive oil
25 g (1 oz) onion, finely chopped
salt and freshly ground black
  pepper

This is a great way to use up leftover potato. Save the porcini water and use it as the stock in a soup or meat recipe. Serve the mash with stews or roast meats.

Soak the porcini for 20 minutes in enough cold water to cover them, then drain and chop roughly.

Meanwhile, boil the potatoes in plenty of salted water. When they are done, drain and mash them (or put through a *passatutto*).

Combine the potatoes, butter, pecorino and milk in a bowl with pepper to taste. If using leftover mash, add a little more milk with the cheese. Heat the olive oil in a frying pan and cook the onions over a gentle heat until golden, then add the mushrooms for 2–3 minutes. Add the mash and fry until hot all the way through.

cannellini bean and rosemary mash

SERVES 4

5 tablespoons extra-virgin olive oil
6 sage leaves
2 sprigs thyme
2 sprigs rosemary
2 × 400 g tins of cannellini beans,
  drained and rinsed
200 ml (7 fl oz) Vegetable Stock
  (page 43), as necessary

This soft herby mash is delicious with Monkfish Cooked with Parsley and White Wine (page 111) and Rack of Lamb in Red Wine, Onions and Rosemary (page 101).

Heat the oil and herbs in a pan for 5 minutes, taking care that they do not burn.

Add the beans and stir well. Cook for 10–15 minutes until the beans are softened and heated through. If they start to dry out, add a little stock.

Remove the herbs and crush the beans briefly with a potato masher.

luciano's roast potatoes

SERVES 4

1 kg (2^1/$_4$ lb) potatoes, peeled and
  cut into walnut-sized chunks
6 tablespoons extra-virgin olive oil
4 sprigs fresh rosemary
6 garlic cloves, unpeeled and
  lightly crushed
salt and freshly ground black
  pepper

Luciano is one of the chefs, and the gardener, at Hotel Le Rotelle in Tuscany. His roast potatoes are the best I have ever eaten – he believes it's the double cooking and his skill at growing rosemary in the herb garden! After the first cooking they can cool completely, so are great for making ahead for dinner parties. Serve with roast meat or fish (see page 113).

Preheat the oven to 200°C/400°F/Gas 6.

Soak the potatoes in water for about 30 minutes. Drain, then dry roughly with a clean tea towel and put into a large roasting tin. Pour over the olive oil and add the rosemary and garlic, and season with salt and pepper. Mix well with your hands. Transfer to the oven and cook for 30–40 minutes until the potatoes are soft inside.

Remove the potatoes from the oven and leave to cool for about 30 minutes. Toss the potatoes well and return them to the oven for another 15 minutes until hot and crispy on the outside.

green beans in tomato sauce

SERVES 4

300 g (11 oz) green string beans
^{1}/$_2$ quantity Basic Tomato Sauce
  (page 64)
salt

Most restaurants serve these as a side dish. They're easy to make and are particularly good served with roast meats.

Top and tail the beans. Bring a pan of salted water to the boil and cook the beans for 5–7 minutes or until al dente. Drain.

Pour the tomato sauce into the pan and add the beans. Heat through for 5 minutes, stirring occasionally, and serve immediately.

stocks

AND SOUPS

vegetable stock • fish stock • chicken stock • beef stock • giancarlo's soffritto • luciano's soffritto • fennel and rosemary soup • chick-pea soup • ribollita • gregorio's chestnut and lentil soup • mixed bean soup • orchard-keepers' soup • fish soup

stocks and soups

We always know the worth of a chef by his stock. Good chefs have at least three large pans of it on the go, made fresh every morning; bad ones have a tower of plastic containers filled with dried bouillon. In a good chef's kitchen there will be fish, meat and vegetable stock and maybe chicken if that is required. I know that the pans would take up an entire hob at home but I urge you to start from scratch next time you need stock, rather than reaching for an over-salted artificial-tasting cube at the back of your cupboard. Natural stock enriches a soup or sauce in a far more satisfying way – you'll never look back.

Next time you make stock, freeze any that's left over in ice-cube trays, then transfer the cubes to a labelled freezer bag. That way you will have perfectly measured small amounts of stock for cooking.

Stock helps minimize waste, since you can use ingredients that might otherwise be thrown away – for example, peelings from vegetables such as carrots, onions and celery. When preparing a vegetable stock be careful not to use anything with too strong a taste, like cabbage, as it will overpower the flavour in the main dish. The more the liquid is reduced during cooking, the more intense the flavour of the stock will be. To make a meat stock, add bones left over from a roast. Fish stock can be made with discarded trimmings: fish heads, tails and fins.

Remember to be generous with the time you allow to make a stock. Choose the ingredients carefully to blend with your finished recipe, and if you feel the flavour is too weak, boil the stock further to reduce it. Never add salt as it could make your final dish too salty.

Soffritto: the essential flavour

Soffritto comes from *soffrigere* (to fry). It refers to finely chopped vegetables and herbs that are fried in olive oil and are the essence, the depth of flavour, of all soups, sauces and stews. No self-respecting Tuscan would cook one of these without a *soffritto* and everyone has a slight twist to the way they make it. Giancarlo's mother used to prepare hers on a wooden board, using a small sharp axe that was really for chopping branches. Over a few years the board would become thinner and thinner and have to be replaced – presumably the family had been eating small pieces of wood with their food! Giancarlo uses only woody herbs in his *soffritto*, Luciano uses fresh parsley at Hotel Le Rotelle. Cinnamon or other spices are sometimes added, or occasionally lemon zest.

La cucina povera

It has to be said that almost every nation believes it makes the best soup. But Italians know good food and they really know how to make good soup! The most inspired recipes in any culture probably come from the cooking of the poor, and Tuscany provides one of the best examples of *la cucina povera* or peasant cooking. A good example is *ribollita* (page 51). This soup was traditionally made with leftover vegetable soup from the day before, which was reboiled – hence its name. It is so delicious, though, that it's worth making it without any leftovers! *Ribollita* would have once provided the whole meal for a family since it's so thick that it is almost like a stew. Today, however, we serve it in the restaurant as a starter. Meat is not an essential ingredient in soup, but the base of all soups is a good *soffritto* followed by a good stock.

Bean soups

'I Toscani soni i mangiafagioli' translates as the rather derisory 'Tuscans are the bean-eaters'. But it's a fact. Classic peasant food, Tuscan soups are usually eaten in winter – hence the use of beans, legumes and grains stored since the summer and of delicious *cavolo nero* (black kale), which grows in cold conditions. Beans such as borlotti, cannellini, fava, *corona* (butter beans), *lenticchie* (lentils) and *ceci* (chick-peas) are common. Tuscan bean soups are generally quite thick. Usually about a third of the beans are put through a *passatutto* (food mill), which helps to thicken the soup, and the rest are left whole and added at the

end for texture. Giancarlo is not a gadget-lover but he wouldn't be without his *passatutto* – every Italian house has one for mashing or puréeing.

Bread soups

Tuscany's saltless bread goes hard very quickly once the loaf is cut. Traditonally, this meant that since nothing was wasted a use had to be found for the mountain of stale bread that was added to every day. One way of using it up was to thicken soups such as *pappa al pomodoro* (bread and tomato soup). Bread is also added to *ribollita* along with vegetables and beans.

Different names for soup

As Italian recipes differ from one region to another, so too do their soup definitions – these are Giancarlo's. *Brodo* or consommé is a thin broth made from meat or chicken. It is fundamental to many sauces, but also traditionally served on its own to someone who is unwell. It is frequently flavoured with parsley, which in Tuscany is very strong, almost as full of flavour as celery. A *minestra* is a thin soup with small pieces of cappelini (tiny pasta stars) or rice in it. A minestrone is thicker and full of vegetables. The name *zuppa* comes from *inzuppare*, meaning to dunk. It is a heavy soup made with vegetables, bread, pasta or beans, and is often a meal on its own. *Crema di zuppa* is a creamed or puréed soup, made by passing the ingredients through a *passatutto*.

Serving suggestions for soup

Giancarlo breaks bread into his soup at the table. I sometimes wish he wouldn't, but I understand why he does – to thicken the soup and because it reminds him of home! There are many ways of serving soup, and lots of accompaniments and extras to make it even more special.

Place a slice of toasted bread on the bottom of a soup bowl. Drizzle with olive oil and scrape with a garlic clove. Pour the hot soup over. The garlic will breathe life back into the hard bread, which will become a wonderful treat like a surprise snack at the bottom of the bowl.

Use up stale bread by toasting it, sprinkling it with grated Parmesan or pecorino and placing it in a soup bowl. Pour in the hot soup and top with a little more cheese grated over the soup.

For a touch of heat rub a fresh red chilli (seeded) over a slice of bread before toasting it, then put the bread on the bottom of a soup bowl and top with the hot soup.

Hollow out a large, crusty roll and serve a thick soup like *ribollita* or lentil soup in it. You can replace the 'lid' before serving, if desired.

Add a drizzle of extra-virgin olive oil to a bowl of soup to add a beautiful shine and flavour.

Sprinkle freshly grated pecorino or Parmesan over the soup just before serving, to add a deliciously tangy, salty flavour.

Finely shred a little lemon zest over the soup for a refreshing zing.

vegetable stock

Delicate stock is perfect for soups and this is a good way to use up leftover vegetables or peelings. Basil and thyme can be added in small quantities, but would be too overpowering in a meat or fish stock. Tie the herbs together with a piece of string so that they don't break up and can be removed easily. The boiled vegetables can be passed through a passatutto *(food mill) to make soup.*

Put all the ingredients into a large pan and cover with 3 litres (5¼ pints) cold water. Bring to the boil, then reduce the heat and simmer for 1 hour. Skim regularly with a slotted spoon to remove any scum. Strain the stock through muslin or a sieve before using.

MAKES 1.75 LITRES (3 PINTS)

1 carrot
2 celery sticks
1 tomato
1 medium onion, unpeeled
1 medium potato
bunch of mixed fresh herbs
   (eg parsley, thyme and basil),
   tied up with string
10 black peppercorns

fish stock

This is the key to any flavoursome fish dish, including Fish Soup (page 56). It is easy to make – you just need to order the fish bones and allow an hour to make the stock. In the UK, as in Italy, the head or bones of any kind of fish will do, but the gills must be removed.

Put all the ingredients into a large pan and cover with 3 litres (5¼ pints) cold water. Bring to the boil, then reduce the heat and simmer for 1 hour. Skim regularly with a slotted spoon.

Strain the stock through muslin or a sieve, then leave it to rest for 1 hour until the sediment has settled. Ladle the stock out, avoiding the sediment.

MAKES 1.75 LITRES (3 PINTS)

1 celery stick
1 carrot
1 fish head
bones from 2 fish
1 medium onion
10 black peppercorns
2 tomatoes
small bunch of fresh parsley

Every chef has his or her own twist on a stock recipe. For his chicken stock Giancarlo prefers, as his mother did, to use an older bird that has stopped laying eggs, as this imparts a stronger flavour. It is a good idea to tie the herbs together with string to stop them breaking up, as they can then be removed more easily. You can use this recipe for many chicken dishes, including Chicken with Cinnamon and Lemon (page 94).

chicken stock

MAKES 2.5 LITRES (4^1/$_4$ PINTS)

1 old chicken (ask your butcher
   for a broiler), weighing about
   1.8 kg (4 lb)
2 carrots
2 celery sticks
2 tomatoes
1 potato
^{1}/$_2$ onion
12 black peppercorns
12 juniper berries (optional),
   gently squeezed
small bunch of fresh parsley
3 bay leaves

Put all the ingredients into a very large pan and cover with 3 litres (5^1/$_4$ pints) cold water. Bring to the boil, then reduce the heat and simmer for 2–3 hours. Skim regularly with a slotted spoon to remove any scum.

Strain the stock through muslin or a sieve, then leave it to rest for 1 hour until the sediment has settled. Ladle the stock out, avoiding the sediment.

Known as brodo di carne *in Italian, this is always on the go in our restaurant kitchens and making it was an essential part of the course in Tuscany. It is a rich meat stock, perfect for* ragus *and sauces.*

beef stock

MAKES 2 LITRES (3$\frac{1}{2}$ PINTS)

1 kg (2$\frac{1}{4}$ lb) beef bones
1 kg (2$\frac{1}{4}$ lb) veal bones
2 carrots
2 celery sticks
2 tomatoes
1 potato
$\frac{1}{2}$ onion
12 black peppercorns
12 juniper berries (optional),
  gently squeezed
small bunch of fresh parsley
3 bay leaves

Put the beef and veal bones in a large pan and add enough cold water to cover them completely. Bring to the boil, then reduce the heat and simmer for about 40 minutes. A lot of fat and scum will be released from the bones. Skim these off regularly with a slotted spoon.

After 40 minutes, remove any remaining scum and add the rest of the ingredients. Bring to the boil again, then reduce the heat and simmer for 3–4 hours.

Strain the stock through muslin or a sieve, then leave it to rest for 1 hour until the sediment has settled. Ladle the stock out, avoiding the sediment.

giancarlo's soffritto

MAKES ABOUT 200 G (7 OZ)

150 ml (½ pint) extra-virgin
   olive oil
1½ red onions, weighing about
   150 g (5 oz), very finely chopped
2 celery sticks, weighing about
   150 g (5 oz), very finely chopped
1 medium carrot, weighing about
   150 g (5 oz), very finely chopped
1 teaspoon salt
2 sprigs fresh rosemary
3 bay leaves
2 garlic cloves, left whole and
   crushed with the flat side of
   a knife
freshly ground black pepper

This is the essential combination of ingredients that forms the basis of any Tuscan soup, stew or casserole. It gives depth of flavour and a herbiness to them. Every cook has their favourite way of making it and will alter it according to the time of year or the finished recipe. It is better to chop the vegetables by hand – a food processor tends to purée the vegetables, making them too watery for a successful soffritto.

Heat the olive oil in a pan and add the onion, celery and carrot, and season with the salt and some pepper. Add the rosemary, bay leaves and garlic and cook over a low heat for 15 minutes, stirring often – this allows the onion to become sweet. Remove the rosemary and bay leaves, and use the *soffritto* in your chosen dish.

(If you are making a dish with a delicate flavour, put the rosemary and garlic into the oil first. After 2 minutes remove and discard them. This keeps their flavour to a hint rather than a blast!)

Luciano at Hotel Le Rotelle has his own herbier version of soffritto. He uses loads of parsley, whereas Giancarlo uses none (see page 46) and their methods are slightly different as well, with Luciano's having a much shorter cooking time. But they agree that you must use plenty of good-quality, extra-virgin olive oil.

luciano's soffritto

MAKES ABOUT 200 G (7 OZ)

100 ml ($3^1/_2$ fl oz) extra-virgin
   olive oil
1 red onion, weighing about 100 g
   (4 oz), finely chopped
large handful of fresh parsley,
   finely chopped
2 celery sticks, weighing about
   150 g (5 oz), finely chopped
1 medium carrot, weighing about
   150 g (5 oz), finely chopped
1 teaspoon salt
leaves from 1 sprig fresh rosemary,
   finely chopped
3 fresh sage leaves, finely chopped
2 garlic cloves, finely chopped
freshly ground black pepper

Heat the olive oil in a pan and add the onion, parsley, celery and carrot, and season with the salt and some pepper.

Add the rosemary, sage and garlic and cook over a low heat for 5 minutes, stirring constantly to prevent the parsley burning. Use the *soffritto* in your chosen dish.

Fennel is very popluar in Tuscany and is used in countless ways. It is thought to be good eaten raw at the end of a meal to aid digestion. This recipe uses puréed fennel, its aniseed flavour complemented by the rosemary. It is a very light soup, but still filling, and therefore great for those who may have overindulged on some of the more fattening recipes in this book! You could add 400 g (14 oz) potatoes, cut into chunks, when cooking the fennel, for a creamier, more velvety texture.

fennel and rosemary soup

**SERVES 6 AS A STARTER
OR 4 AS A MAIN COURSE**

4 heads of fennel, trimmed and
  washed
1 quantity *soffritto* ingredients
  (page 46 or 48)
1.5 litres (2$^1/_2$ pints) Vegetable
  Stock (page 43)
extra-virgin olive oil, for drizzling
leaves from 1 sprig fresh rosemary,
  finely chopped
1 quantity Tuscan Garlic Bread
  (page 24)

Cut each fennel head into four. Boil in salted water for 15 minutes.

Meanwhile, cook the *soffritto* as on page 46 or 48.

When the fennel is cooked, drain and chop finely. Add to the *soffritto* and cook for a further 5 minutes.

Add the stock and cook for 20 minutes.

Put the soup through a *passatutto* (food mill) or blender. Drizzle with olive oil, sprinkle with rosemary, and serve, accompanied by hot slices of Tuscan garlic bread.

This is a typical Tuscan soup. A little cooked pasta, such as penne, is sometimes added at the end of cooking to make it more of a substantial meal. Allow two days to make the soup as the chick-peas need to soak overnight. If you are in a hurry, use canned chick-peas, which don't require soaking. For a vegetarian version, leave out the prosciutto and replace the chicken stock with Vegetable Stock (page 43).

chick-pea soup

SERVES 6

500 g (1 lb 2 oz) dried chick-peas
  or 3 × 410 g tins
1 carrot
1 tomato
1 bay leaf
1 celery stick
1 quantity *soffritto* ingredients
  (page 46 or 48)
100 g (4 oz) prosciutto, pancetta
  or ham, in one piece
2 litres (3$^1/_2$ pints) Chicken Stock
  (page 44)
Quick Focaccia (page 144), to serve

Soak the chick-peas overnight in 1 litre (1$^3/_4$ pints) cold water.

Drain the chick-peas and discard the soaking water. Rinse them thoroughly in cold water. Put them into a large pan and cover with cold water. Add the carrot, tomato, bay leaf and celery and bring to the boil. Reduce the heat and simmer, covererd, for 1$^1/_2$–2 hours. When the chick-peas are soft to the touch, they are done.

Cook the *soffritto* as on page 46 or 48. Cook the garlic and herbs in the oil first, along with the meat, but don't discard them when you add the remaining ingredients.

Add three-quarters of the chick-peas, reserving the remainder in the cooking liquid to keep warm. Add the stock and simmer for another 30 minutes.

Remove the rosemary, bay leaves and meat, and pass the soup through a *passatutto* (food mill), or process it until it is smooth and velvety.

Return to a clean pan and heat gently for 10 minutes until piping hot. Serve in warm bowls, with the whole chick-peas scattered on top, and accompanied by focaccia.

One of the most popular soups in Tuscany, this uses a roughly chopped, rustic soffritto, *which gives the finished soup a really chunky texture. Adding slices of bread at the end makes it filling and a meal in its own right. It is a classic peasant recipe.*

ribollita

SERVES 6

200 ml (7 fl oz) olive oil

2 garlic cloves – 1 chopped

100 g (4 oz) white onions, roughly chopped

300 g (11 oz) carrots, roughly chopped

300 g (11 oz) celery, roughly chopped

400 g (14 oz) courgettes, roughly chopped

300 g (11 oz) Savoy cabbage, roughly chopped

300g (11 oz) black kale (*cavolo nero*), roughly chopped

200g (7 oz) spinach, chopped

550 g (1¼ lb) potatoes, roughly chopped

100 g (4 oz) tomatoes, peeled and chopped

800 g (1¾ lb) cooked cannellini beans, or 2 × 400 g cans

1 litre (1¾ pints) Vegetable Stock (page 43)

1 white farmhouse loaf

extra-virgin olive oil, for drizzling

salt and freshly ground black pepper

freshly grated pecorino, to serve

Heat the olive oil in a large pan and add the chopped garlic and onions. Cook gently until the onions are soft. Add the carrots, celery, and season with salt and pepper. Cook over a low heat for a further 15 minutes until this *soffritto* turns golden, stirring occasionally.

Once the *soffritto* is ready, add the courgettes, Savoy cabbage, black kale and spinach. Leave to sweat for about 10 minutes, then add the potatoes and tomatoes. Mash half the cannellini beans and stir into the pan. Cook gently for about 5 minutes.

Add the stock and simmer, covered, for 30 minutes, stirring regularly. About 10 minutes before the end of cooking, add the remaining cannellini beans. Preheat the oven to 160°C/325°F/Gas 3.

Cut the bread into slices and toast them in the oven (or use the grill or a toaster). Rub each slice with the whole garlic clove and drizzle with a little extra-virgin olive oil.

Place a layer of toast in the bottom of a shallow ovenproof lasagne dish and pour over some of the soup. Repeat until all the toast and soup have been used.

Let the soup stand for a while before serving. Alternatively the soup can be kept warm, uncovered, in the oven for up to 15 minutes. If you put the *ribollita* in the oven, make sure all the toast is covered by soup, or it will burn.

Serve in warm bowls, drizzled with extra-virgin olive oil and scattered with pecorino.

Tuscany is well known for its hearty lentil soups. Gregorio Piazza, our head chef, regularly makes this one in winter. I love the texture of the chestnuts and lentils. The soup is very filling, so it makes a good lunch served with hot crusty bread.

gregorio's chestnut and lentil soup

**SERVES 6 AS A STARTER
OR 4 AS A MAIN COURSE**

150 g (5 oz) chestnuts
1 quantity *soffritto* ingredients
    (page 46 or 48)
500 g (1 lb 2 oz) green lentils
200 g can chopped tomatoes
1.5 –2 litres (2¹/₂–3¹/₂ pints)
    Vegetable Stock (page 43) or
    Chicken Stock (page 44)
extra-virgin olive oil, for drizzling

Preheat the oven to 200°C/400°F/Gas 6.

Using a small, sharp knife, make a small cross in the top of each chestnut – this will stop them exploding in the oven. Place the chestnuts on a baking sheet and roast them for 15 minutes.

Let them cool a little, then peel and roughly chop two-thirds of them, keeping the remainder whole for decoration.

Meanwhile, cook the *soffritto* as on page 46 or 48.

Add the lentils and chopped chestnuts to the *soffritto* once it's ready. Stir for 5 minutes to combine all the ingredients thoroughly.

Add the tomatoes and stock. Bring to a simmer, then cook for 2 hours, uncovered, stirring frequently.

About 5 minutes before the soup is ready, pass a third of the soup through a *passatutto* (food mill) or sieve. Discard the skins of the lentils that are left behind. Return the sieved soup to the pan and bring to the boil.

Divide the soup between four or six warm bowls, depending on whether you're serving it for a starter or a main course. Scatter with the whole chestnuts and drizzle with extra-virgin olive oil.

The Tuscans are often mocked by other Italians because they eat so many beans. These grow well in Tuscany and in summer are often eaten fresh and raw, with cheese. Thrifty Tuscan housewives know how to dry and preserve them so that they can also be enjoyed in winter. Beans soups are filling, tasty and inexpensive to make. This ones uses the tail end of a prosciutto bone to enhance the flavour, but you can replace it with ham or a veal bone, and vegetarians can leave it out altogether. Allow two days to make this soup as the beans need to soak overnight.

mixed bean soup

SERVES 8

300 g (11 oz) dried cannelllini beans
300 g (11 oz) dried borlotti beans
300 g (11 oz) dried kidney beans
1 quantity *soffritto* ingredients (page 46 or 48)
100 g (4 oz) prosciutto bone
1 litre (1$\frac{3}{4}$ pints) Chicken Stock (page 44) or Vegetable Stock (page 43)
salt and freshly ground black pepper
extra-virgin olive oil, for drizzling
freshly grated pecorino, to serve

Place each type of bean in a separate bowl, cover with cold water and leave to soak overnight.

Rinse the beans thoroughly and drain. Place each type of bean in a separate pan and cover with water. Bring to the boil, cover, and cook the cannellini beans for 45 minutes, the borlotti beans for 1 hour and the kidney beans for 1$\frac{1}{4}$ hours. Drain and set aside.

Cook the *soffritto* as on page 46 or 48. Cook the garlic and herbs in the oil first, along with the prosciutto bone, but don't discard them when you add the remaining ingredients.

Add three-quarters of the beans and reserve the remainder. Season to taste with salt and pepper, and cook for a further 10 minutes, stirring carefully so as not to break up the beans.

Add the stock, bring to the boil, then reduce the heat and simmer, covered, for a further 25 minutes.

Stir in the whole beans. Taste and adjust the seasoning, if necessary.

Serve in warm bowls, drizzled with extra-virgin olive oil and scattered with pecorino.

An ortolano *is a keeper of an* orto, *or plot of land used for growing – I suppose the closest English equivalent would be an orchard-keeper or allotment-holder. This soup,* zuppa al ortolana, *is named after the* ortolani, *who make the most of their vegetables all year round – even ones that have fallen to the ground at the end of the season.*

orchard-keepers' soup

SERVES 6

1 quantity Luciano's Soffritto
  (page 48)
200 g (7 oz) carrots, diced
200 g (7 oz) celery, diced
200 g (7 oz) potatoes, diced
200 g (7 oz) courgettes, diced
1.5 litres (2$\frac{1}{4}$ pints) Vegetable
  Stock (page 43)
2 tomatoes, peeled and diced,
  with juice and pips squeezed out
salt and freshly ground black
  pepper
freshly grated pecorino, to serve

Cook the *soffritto* as on page 48.

Add the vegetables to the *soffritto* once it's ready and cook over a low heat for 10–15 minutes, stirring continuously but gently – they musn't break up too much. Season to taste with salt and pepper.

Add the stock and cook over a low heat, partially covered for 30–40 minutes. Add the tomatoes for the last 10 minutes of the cooking time .

Serve in warm bowls, scattered with pecorino and sprinkled with a little more pepper.

As a child, living inland in Tuscany, Giancarlo rarely ate shellfish, although occasionally there were mussels from the local river. However, he loves seafood, as do our children. Enjoy big bowls of this soup with crusty white bread. The mussels and clams give a delicious salty flavour.

fish soup

SERVES 6

6 tablespoons olive oil
1/2 large or 1 small red onion, finely chopped
2 garlic cloves
1/2 teaspoon chilli powder (optional)
1 small squid, cleaned
300 g (11 oz) monkfish, cleaned
200 ml (7 fl oz) white wine
400 g can chopped tomatoes
300 g (11 oz) live clams, scrubbed and beards removed (see pages 105–6)
300 g (11 oz) live mussels, scrubbed and beards removed (see pages 105–6)
12 king or tiger prawns, shells on
1 litre (1 3/4 pints) Fish Stock (page 43)
salt and freshly ground black pepper
small handful of fresh parsley, torn, to garnish
crusty white bread, to serve

Heat the oil in a large pan and fry the onion over a medium heat for 5–7 minutes, until golden. Add the garlic and cook for about 1 minute, taking care not to burn it. Season with salt and pepper, and stir in the chilli powder, if using.

Add the squid and monkfish and fry for 5 minutes. Then stir in the wine and cook for about 3 minutes until it has reduced.

Add the tomatoes, bash them with a wooden spoon to break them up a bit (they will also break down during cooking) and cook for 10 minutes.

Add the clams, mussels, prawns and stock and bring to the boil. Reduce the heat and simmer, uncovered, for about 20 minutes. At this point discard any closed clams and mussels – do not force them open.

Taste to adjust the seasoning, then serve in warm bowls, garnished with parsley and accompanied by crusty bread.

pasta

FRESH AND DRIED

pasta

When I was getting to know Giancarlo, I cheekily took some pasta from his plate to try it. He snapped at me and said there are two things you never take from an Italian man: his woman and his pasta. He meant it. Now I order my own if I want it! Giancarlo, like most Italians, needs his pasta every day. We have even taken it with us on holiday in case we can't buy any when we reach our destination.

Pasta is essential to all Tuscans. A Tuscan without pasta is like an English person without tea. It is eaten at least once a day and usually precedes the main course.

Fresh versus dried pasta

The two main types of pasta are fresh, usually made by hand, and dried, usually made by machine. Fresh pasta is made with 00 finely ground soft wheat flour and eggs. Dried pasta is made with semolina (a hard wheat flour) and water. Fresh pasta is usually made into long ribbons, from fine *tagliolini* to medium tagliatelle and wide pappardelle, and is also used for stuffed pastas such as ravioli and *tortelloni*. Unless it is made and sold on the same day, I wouldn't recommend buying fresh pasta from a shop. Spaghetti, linguine, fusilli and farfalle, along with hollow pasta shapes such as penne or rigatoni, are always machine-made and all are sold dried.

Some dishes simply work better with fresh pasta and others are best with dried. Italians would not consider either type to be better than the other.

Which sauce, which pasta?

Fresh pasta is made on wood and has a rougher surface because of the pattern of the wood, which can't be seen with the naked eye. Because dried pasta is made by a machine it has a very smooth texture as it has been pressed against metal. Fresh pasta is the more permeable of the two, and therefore absorbs more flavour with 'drier' sauces, such as the rich meat *ragus* of Tuscany. Dried pasta is better with ingredients, like seafood, that require a more liquid sauce that would be too quickly absorbed by fresh pasta. We prefer using the fresh type for lasagne, but dried works well if you blanch it first – however, we don't believe in the 'no-cook' variety.

In Italy pasta comes in all shapes, sizes and colours. There is green pasta made with spinach (*pasta verde*), black made with squid ink (*pasta al nero di seppia*) and red which uses tomato purée (*pasta pomodoro*). Each type has its roots firmly in a particular region. Examples are wide strips of pappardelle or fettucine, and narrow ribbons of *pici* from Tuscany; *orrechiete* (little ears) from Puglia; and the short, rolled beads of *trenette* from Liguria. Each blends perfectly with traditional sauces, which are nearly always made from local ingredients.

When and what is al dente?

Pasta should be cooked in plenty of hot, rapidly boiling, salted water. Fresh pasta cooks quickly, usually in 3–4 minutes. Dried takes longer, usually 9–12 minutes, but follow the instructions on the packet. Check if the pasta is ready when it comes to the surface. In Italy pasta is eaten al dente, literally 'to the tooth', which is often too hard for non-Italians. It should have a little bite to it and not be soft enough for you to squash it with your tongue.

Remove the pasta from the water as soon as it is cooked and drain it. At this point pour the sauce over the pasta and toss well, then serve immediately in warm bowls.

How to reheat pasta

If you have anything left over from a pasta dish, cover it in cling film once it has cooled and keep it in the fridge overnight. The next day, reheat small portions, also covered in cling film, in the microwave. Alternatively, put the pasta in a frying pan, add a small amount of stock – just enough to stop it sticking – and cook, stirring frequently, until it is heated through. Giancarlo believes the flavour of pasta with a meat *ragu* is even better the following day.

How to store fresh pasta

A ball of fresh pasta dough wrapped in cling film can be stored in the fridge for up to three days. If you want to store the pasta once it has been rolled and shaped, hang ribbons over a wooden pole to dry, or spread sheets out on tea towels. Once dry, put the pasta into a basket and use within four to five days. Make sure there is plenty of air circulating around it.

Stuffed pasta, such as ravioli and *tortelloni,* can be frozen. Place a single layer of the sheets on a tray sprinkled with flour or, preferably, semolina. Make sure they don't touch one another while they freeze. Once frozen, the shapes can be put into plastic bags and stored for up to six months. To cook the frozen pasta, allow a minute longer than normal as the heat of the water needs to pass into the frozen fillings.

Giancarlo's fresh pasta recipe

Making fresh pasta can be time consuming but once you've tried your own home-made version you'll never look back!

**MAKES ENOUGH PASTA FOR 6
(OR 8 STARTER PORTIONS)**

700 g (1½ lb) 00 flour
5 medium-sized free-range eggs, preferably from
  corn-fed hens (for colour)

Pour the flour on to a flat wooden surface to make a mound, and make a well in the centre of the mound. Crack the eggs into the well and use a blunt knife or your hands to gradually mix the eggs and flour together. When the mixture in the centre of the mound has become a thick paste, use your hands to incorporate more flour. You could use a food processor, which will require less kneading by hand, but this will affect the finished result. To obtain genuine, home-made pasta with its unique texture you should use your hands. Their warmth and a wooden work surface provide something special that no food processor or metallic surface can match. Kneading by hand is very therapeutic, too.

When you have a ball of dough but there are still lots of small crumbs, incorporate the wetter crumbs in the dough. Sieve the drier ones and the remaining flour (don't expect to use up all the flour). Discard the crumbs and use the sifted flour while you are kneading the dough, to stop it sticking to your hands and the work surface. Be careful – don't add too much flour and make the dough too dry. It is ready when it forms a soft, firm but flexible ball and springs back when you touch it.

Leave it to rest for about 20 minutes – invert a bowl over the dough or cover it with cling film. This prevents it drying out while it is resting and relaxes the gluten strands in the flour, making it easier to roll out the dough. If any flour is left over, sieve it again to remove the crumbs and save it for rolling out the dough. Giancarlo's mother reused the left-over bits in soups.

After resting, the dough can be rolled out using a rolling pin or a pasta machine. To prevent it drying out, divide it in half before rolling, and wrap the half you're not using in cling film. When cut open, the ball of dough will be spongy with pockets of air trapped inside.

To make long pasta such as tagliatelle or pappardelle, roll the dough out using a heavy, wooden rolling pin. Dust the work surface, the dough and the rolling pin with flour to prevent sticking. Begin by flattening the dough with the palm of your hand, then place the rolling pin across the top of the dough and roll it towards the centre. Continue rolling the pin backwards and forwards, turning the dough every so often. The dough should spread out and flatten evenly. When it is thin enough for you to see your fingers through it (about 1 mm/ 1/16 in), roll it up like a flattened cigar, from one edge to the centre, then from the other edge to the centre. Make sure it is well floured. Cut into the desired thickness to make *pasta lunga* (long pasta), the thinnest being *tagliolini* and the fattest pappardelle.

Pull the pasta out into individual strands, and toss them with semolina or a little more flour to prevent them sticking. Leave on a floured tray. Repeat with the remaining dough and cook within the hour.

Cook the pasta in boiling salted water for 3–5 minutes, depending on the thickness of the strands. To see if it's ready, taste a strand – if you have to bite it, it needs another minute or two.

This is the essential tomato sauce for dressing pasta and the basis for a whole range of other dishes. It can be kept in the fridge for a few days, so we always make loads of it. The sauce can be used in a variety of ways. We even eat it for breakfast, when we heat it in a frying pan and crack a few eggs over the top, to cook in the hot tomatoes – this was Giancarlo's father's favourite dish. Serve with crusty bread for mopping up the juices. If you're serving the sauce with pasta, drain the pasta and add it to the hot sauce. Toss well, pour into warm bowls, top with Parmesan and basil, and serve.

basic tomato sauce

SERVES 4

6–8 tablespoons olive oil
½ large or 1 small red onion,
  finely chopped
2 garlic cloves
2 × 400 g cans chopped tomatoes
200 ml (7 fl oz) Vegetable Stock
  (page 43)
salt and freshly ground black
  pepper

Heat the olive oil in a pan and fry the onion over a medium heat for 5–7 minutes until golden. Add the garlic and cook for about 1 minute, taking care not to burn the garlic. Add the salt and pepper.

Add the tomatoes, and bash them with a wooden spoon to break them up a bit (they will also break down during cooking). Add the stock to the pan.

Reduce the heat and simmer, uncovered, for about 40 minutes. The sauce should be thick and not watery, so allow it to reduce. This will concentrate the flavours. If it tastes a bit too tangy add more stock and simmer a bit longer, allowing the tomatoes to cook thoroughly. Adding stock ensures that the sauce won't catch on the pan and burn. Adjust the seasoning to taste before serving.

In Tuscany this is called sugo di nana *(duck sauce) –* nana *is short for* anatra *(duck). It is served with home-made pasta ribbons such as tagliatelle or pappardelle and a little freshly grated Parmesan or pecorino. Duck is very popular in Tuscany and many families keep their own. Some years ago, the noise of the ducks became so annoying that a new breed – the* nana muta *– was introduced, whose quack was quieter than most.*

duck ragu

SERVES 6–8

1 quantity *soffritto* ingredients
   (page 46 or 48)
1 duck weighing approximately
   2.5 kg (5$^{1}/_{2}$ lb), jointed and cut
   into pieces the size of a small fist
plain flour, for dredging
3 tablespoons olive oil
100 ml (3$^{1}/_{2}$ fl oz) red wine
2 tablespoons tomato purée
500 g (1 lb 2 oz) canned tomatoes,
   chopped
1 litre (1$^{3}/_{4}$ pints) Chicken Stock
   (see page 44), plus a little extra,
   if necessary
salt and freshly ground black
   pepper

First, cook the *soffritto* as on page 46 or 48.

Meanwhile, remove any obvious pieces of fat from the duck joints. Put the flour and seasoning in a shallow bowl and mix well. Roll the duck pieces in the flour to coat. Heat the olive oil in a large frying pan and fry the duck in batches over a medium heat for 3 minutes on each side until golden and crispy. Set aside on kitchen paper to drain.

Add the duck pieces to the *soffritto* and cook over a medium heat for 5 minutes, stirring constantly. Add the wine and reduce for a couple of minutes. Add the tomato purée, tomatoes and stock, and stir well. Reduce the heat a little and cook, partially covered, for about 1 hour until the duck is cooked through. Stir occasionally.

Remove the duck pieces from the pan and allow to cool for about 15 minutes. Leave the sauce simmering gently, uncovered, while you remove the meat from the bones and tear or chop into small pieces. Discard the skin and bones. Return the meat to the sauce and bring back to the boil. Reduce the heat and simmer for 10 minutes. If the sauce is still too runny, let it reduce for a further 10 minutes. If it becomes too dry, add a bit more stock. Taste and adjust the seasoning, if necessary, before serving.

pici

SERVES 4

1 kg (2¼ lb) 00 flour
pinch of salt
1 egg
2 tablespoons extra-virgin olive oil

Giancarlo's mother often made this classic peasant pasta from Montepulciano as it is economical and money was short. Pici are fun, but quite time consuming to make. Serve them with Arrabbiata Sauce (page 68) or Meat Ragu (page 74).

Mix the flour and salt together on a flat surface. Make a well in the centre of the flour and break the egg into it. Gradually mix the egg and flour together with a knife. Then gradually add about 500 ml (18 fl oz) cold water (you may not need all of it). Knead until well blended. The dough should feel flexible but firm.

Roll out the dough with a rolling pin until it measures about 45 × 45 cm (18 × 18 in) and is 1 cm (½ in) thick. Pour the olive oil over and spread evenly. Cut the dough into strips 1 × 1 cm (½ × ½ in) wide. Leave to rest for 20 minutes.

Use your hands to roll the strips into rounded *pici*, pulling as you roll. They should be like thick lengths of spaghetti.

To cook, bring a large pan of salted water to the boil and cook for about 10–12 minutes.

This classic spicy sauce is simple to make and our students often asked for it as it is so quick to prepare and the ingredients are usually to hand. We serve ours with home-made Pici (page 66) but it is equally peppery and delicious over hot spaghetti, with a sprinkling of grated Parmesan. The chillies in our restaurant vary in heat, even though we buy them from the same supplier. If yours are very spicy, go easy with them.

arrabbiata sauce

**SERVES 6 AS A STARTER
OR 4 AS A MAIN COURSE**

5 tablespoons olive oil
1 red onion, finely chopped
1–2 fresh red chillies (depending
   on how spicy you like your food),
   seeded and roughly chopped
2 × 400 g cans chopped tomatoes
1 garlic clove, crushed
salt and freshly ground black
   pepper

Heat the olive oil in a pan and fry the onion over a medium heat until it is soft – about 7 minutes. This sweetens the onion and balances the acidity of the tomatoes in the finished sauce. Add the chilli(es) and fry for 1 minute until softened.

Season generously with salt and pepper and mix well. Add the tomatoes and crushed garlic.

Simmer for 15–20 minutes, uncovered, until the sauce is reduced. Taste to check the seasoning and adjust, if necessary.

pino's tagliatelle
with radicchio, truffle and sausage

**SERVES 6 AS A STARTER
OR 4–6 AS A MAIN COURSE**

1 radicchio
50 ml (2 fl oz) olive oil
1 small red onion, finely chopped
1 fresh red chilli, seeded and
   finely chopped
4 pork sausages, skin removed
   and meat crumbled
125 ml (4$^{1}/_{2}$ fl oz) red wine
2 tablespoons balsamic vinegar
1 tablespoon truffle paste, or to
   taste; or 2 teaspoons truffle oil,
   plus extra to serve (optional)
300–450 g (11 oz–1 lb) dried
   tagliatelle
salt and freshly ground black
   pepper

During our summer in Tuscany we got to know Pino, an enthusiatic Sicilian who runs a restaurant – La Crypta in Torrita di Sienna – with his brothers. We took our students there for dinner and they loved this dish so much that we persuaded him to give us the recipe. It has a beautiful purplish colour from the cooked radicchio and I think of it as a warming winter dish. Use best-quality sausages with a high meat content. Tuscan sausages are very meaty and lean, and heavy on garlic and salt. Truffle paste and oil are often available in delicatessens.

Cut the radicchio into long, fine strips, reserving a few whole leaves for a garnish. Heat the olive oil in a large non-stick frying pan, and add the onion and cook over a medium heat until soft – about 3 minutes. Add the chilli and continue to cook over a medium heat until the onion starts to brown lightly. Add the sausage meat and cook for about 5 minutes, until browned. Add the radicchio strips and cook for a further 2 minutes. Season with salt and pepper.

Add the wine and vinegar and cook for a further 2 minutes until the liquid has reduced. Stir in the truffle paste or oil and set aside.

Bring a large pan of salted water to the boil. Add the tagliatelle and cook until al dente. Don't overcook the tagliatelle as it will finish cooking in the pan with the sauce. Drain.

Mix the pasta into the sauce straight away and combine thoroughly so that the sauce is heated through. Garnish with the reserved radicchio leaves and serve with extra truffle oil, if desired.

mussel and clam spaghetti
with fresh tomato salsa

SERVES 6 AS A STARTER
OR 4 AS A MAIN COURSE

250 g (9 oz) dried spaghetti
5 tablespoons olive oil
1 medium onion, finely chopped
800 g (1¾ lb) live clams,
  scrubbed and beards removed
  (see pages 105–6)
800 g (1¾ lb) live mussels,
  scrubbed and beards removed
  (see pages 105–6)
1 garlic clove, finely chopped
1 fresh red chilli, seeded and cut
  into thin rings
100 ml (3½ fl oz) white wine
knob of butter
400 g (14 oz) unpeeled tiger or
  king prawns, shells on (optional)
salt and freshly ground black
  pepper
fresh parsley, torn, to garnish
  (optional)

FOR THE TOMATO SALSA
500 g (1 lb 2 oz) very ripe, but not
  slushy, plum or cherry tomatoes,
  diced
pinch of sea salt
handful of fresh basil leaves, torn
  into small pieces
4 garlic cloves, crushed
2 tablespoons extra-virgin olive oil
freshly ground black pepper

Our son, Giorgio, loves spaghetti vongole (spaghetti with clams), and uses an empty shell as pincers to get at the other shellfish hiding in their shells. The idea of adding fresh tomato sauce came from our friend Gino Borella, who was head chef at San Lorenzo in Knightsbridge for 25 years. The sweetness of the garlicky tomato salsa combines wonderfully with the saltiness of the seafood. If I'm really hungry I leave the prawns out, as stopping to peel them slows me down too much!

First make the tomato salsa. Place the tomatoes in a colander and add the sea salt – this helps any excess liquid to drain from the tomatoes. When the liquid has drained away, place the tomatoes in a bowl, add the basil and garlic, and pepper to taste, and cover with olive oil. This can be done a few hours in advance.

Bring a large pan of salted water to the boil. Add the spaghetti and cook according to the packet instructions until al dente. Drain.

Meanwhile, heat the olive oil in a large pan and fry the onion over a medium heat until golden brown. Add the clams and mussels with the garlic, chilli, and wine, and season with salt and pepper. Reduce for a couple of minutes. Add the butter and mix well. Then add the prawns, if using. Cook for a few minutes until the clams and mussels open and the prawns turn pink.

Discard any unopened clams or mussels and mix the seafood into the cooked spaghetti. Divide among warm plates and garnish with parsley if you wish.

Put a spoonful of tomato salsa on each plate so that your guests can mix it into the pasta themselves. Serve any extra at the table.

Many of our students were keen to make gnocchi and were surprised to see how easy it was. Others were convinced that they didn't like them as they had previously eaten hard or rubbery versions. Giancarlo uses white potatoes that are neither too floury or too waxy. He passes them through a passatutto (food mill) and swears this makes a difference as the air is trapped inside making the gnocchi light and airy. As the passatutto is used so much in Tuscan cookery, it is definitely a worthwhile investment. Uncooked gnocchi can be frozen and this sometimes gives an even better result than using fresh ones, as they hold their shape better when they are cooked.

giancarlo's gnocchi

SERVES 8

1 kg (2¼ lb) potatoes
  (King Edward's work well),
  unpeeled
1 egg
300 g (11 oz) 00 flour
1 teaspoon salt

Bring a large pan of water to the boil and cook the potatoes until tender. Peel them while they are still hot and pass them through a *passatutto* (food mill), or use a potato masher. Place in a bowl.

Stir in the egg and flour to form a soft, pliable dough.

Divide the dough into pieces the size of a small fist and roll them out into lengths about 2 cm (¾ in) thick. Cut the lengths into 2 cm (¾ in) long pieces.

Bring a large pan of salted water to the boil and add the gnocchi. When they're cooked they will bob up to the surface – about 2 minutes. Drain well and toss into a sauce such as Sausage and Porcini Sauce (opposite). Serve immediately.

To freeze uncooked gnocchi, spread them out on a well-floured tray, making sure they don't touch each other, and put them in the freezer. When frozen, shake off any excess flour and transfer to a freezer bag. Use within 3 months. Cook from frozen, allowing 1–2 minutes extra cooking time.

sausage and porcini sauce

SERVES 8

5 tablespoons olive oil
1 red onion, finely chopped
500 g (1 lb 2 oz) lean pork
    sausages, skinned and crumbled
3 garlic cloves, left whole and
    crushed
$^1/_2$ fresh red chilli, seeded and
    thinly sliced
3–4 tablespoons dry white wine
50 g (2 oz) dried porcini, covered
    in warm water and soaked for
    20 minutes
150 ml (5 fl oz) double cream
freshly ground black pepper
Giancarlo's Gnocchi (opposite),
    to serve

In Tuscany we use locally made sausages in this delicious sauce for freshly made gnocchi. They are made with very lean meat, so there is not much fat in them. If you cannot get good-quality lean sausages, use pork mince instead.

Heat 3 tablespoons of olive oil in a pan and fry the onion gently until golden. Add the sausagemeat, garlic, chilli and wine and cook over a medium heat for a few minutes until the meat is browned.

Meanwhile, drain and roughly chop the porcini. (Reserve the mushroom water for a soup or stock, if you like.) Heat the remaining oil in a frying pan and cook the porcini with a little pepper.

When the sausage mixture is cooked, add the porcini and cream and stir until the sauce is heated through. Serve with Giancarlo's Gnocchi.

Giancarlo's favourite ragu *is made with a mixture of pork and beef mince. It is how his father made it and how his father's mother made it and, as Tuscans don't like to play around with recipes, this is how it has stayed. Woe betide our children if they think of making it another way! Giancarlo likes to use red onion where possible as it has a sweeter flavour. He makes all our students smell a* ragu *at the beginning of its cooking, halfway through and at the end. This is how he knows it is ready, even without tasting it.*

meat ragu

SERVES 8

1 quantity *soffritto* ingredients
   (page 46 or 48)
750 g (1 lb 10 oz) beef mince
300 g (11 oz) pork mince (the best
   quality you can buy)
400 ml (14 fl oz) red wine
100 ml (3$^{1}/_{2}$ fl oz) Chicken Stock
   (page 44) or Beef Stock
   (page 45), plus extra if necessary
2 × 400 g cans chopped tomatoes
salt and freshly ground black
   pepper

Cook the *soffritto* as on page 46 or 48. When it's ready, add the beef and pork mince and continue to cook until all the liquid from the meat has been absorbed. Keep stirring so that the mince doesn't stick to the bottom. When no more liquid is left add the wine and stir well. Sniff the sauce to see how strong the wine smells – it will change when it is cooked. Simmer over a low heat, uncovered, for 45 minutes.

Warm the stock to avoid lowering the temperature of the *ragu* and add it to the pan with the tomatoes. Stir well. At this point you'll be able to smell a wonderful mixture of flavours – first tomatoes, then meat, then wine.

Leave uncovered and simmer for about 2 hours. Top up the level of liquid with a little more warm stock if the *ragu* starts to dry out. Taste and adjust the seasoning if necessary. At the end of the cooking time, smell the *ragu* again – no single ingredient should dominate.

Discard the rosemary before serving. Use the *ragu* straight away, or cool and transfer to plastic containers for freezing. Use within three months.

Giancarlo's mother made this version of lasagne when she had no ragu to hand. It's a variation on the classic dish and uses just white ingredients – cheese, Béchamel sauce and pasta – hence its name. You could combine various cheeses – try using Gorgonzola or fontina as well as mozzarella. Giancarlo makes the lasagne in three layers in a large roasting tin. It is quick to prepare as there is no ragu to make.

white lasagne

SERVES 6–8

14 sheets fresh lasagne, each
    about 15 × 10 cm (6 × 4 in)
300 g (11 oz) mozzarella, cut into
    small cubes
120 g (4$^{1}/_{2}$ oz) Parmesan, grated
25 g (1 oz) butter, cut into small
    cubes
freshly ground black pepper

FOR THE BÉCHAMEL SAUCE
1 litre (1$^{3}/_{4}$ pints) milk
$^{1}/_{2}$ onion
pinch of freshly grated nutmeg
2 bay leaves
50 g (2 oz) butter
50 g (2 oz) plain flour
salt and freshly ground black
    pepper

Preheat the oven to 180°C/350°F/Gas 4. To make the Béchamel sauce, bring the milk to the boil in a pan with the onion, nutmeg and bay leaves, and season with salt and pepper. Meanwhile, melt the butter in another pan. Stir in the flour and cook for 1–2 minutes, stirring constantly with a wooden spoon. Remove from the heat. Slowly add the flour and butter paste to the hot milk, whisking constantly. Beat well and set aside.

Bring a large pan of salted water to the boil and cook the pasta for 3 minutes.

Pour one-third of the sauce into the bottom of a 30 × 23 × 7.5 cm (12 × 9 × 3 in) ovenproof dish. Top with one-third of the pasta and one-third of the mozzarella and Parmesan. Season generously with black pepper. Repeat this step twice until all the sauce, pasta and cheese have been used up.

Sprinkle the butter over the surface and cook for 30 minutes.

variations

Classic meat lasagne: divide 1 quantity Meat Ragu (opposite) between the layers of cheese and pasta.

Cheese and tomato lasagne: divide 1 quantity Basic Tomato Sauce (page 64) between the layers of cheese and pasta.

We were shown this dish by our friend Franca Buonamici, who is a pastaiola (pasta-maker) at the Buca di Sant' Antonio restaurant in Lucca, Tuscany. Mantovana is one of her specialities – a delicious roll of pasta filled with a variety of stuffings.

mantovana

Put the spinach, ricotta, three-quarters of the Parmesan, nutmeg and seasoning into a large bowl and mix. Taste and add more seasoning, if necessary.

Prepare the pasta dough as on page 62. After it has rested for 20 minutes or so, roll the dough out on a floured surface into a large, flat pancake shape, 2 mm ($^1/_8$ in) thick. Lay a clean tea towel alongside it and make sure the dough isn't any bigger – trim it if it is.

Put enough salted water into a fish kettle or very large saucepan to reach the three-quarters level and bring to the boil.

Meanwhile, spread the spinach and ricotta mixture over the dough, leaving a 2.5 cm (1 in) gap around the outside. Scatter the ham and mozzarella evenly over the surface.

Roll the dough up like a tight Swiss roll, and transfer it carefully to the tea towel. Roll the towel around the dough twice, or use two towels. Secure the roll with string, at both ends and twice along its length, to keep the towel tight. The filling must not escape from the roll.

When the salted water is boiling, lower the mantovana into it. Simmer, uncovered, for 25 minutes. Meanwhile, preheat the oven to 200°C/400°F/Gas 6.

Pour half the tomato sauce and half the Béchamel sauce into an ovenproof dish. Remove the mantovana from the water, untie the string and unroll the tea towel. Cut into slices and place on top of the sauces. Cover the slices with the rest of the tomato and Béchamel sauces, and sprinkle the remaining Parmesan over. Bake in the oven for 10–15 minutes until the cheese is golden and the mantovana is piping hot.

SERVES 6–8

FOR THE PASTA
550 g (1$^1/_4$ lb) flour
3 eggs

FOR THE STUFFING
275 g (10 oz) cooked spinach,
   drained, squeezed and chopped
1 kg (2$^1/_4$ lb) ricotta
80 g (3 oz) Parmesan, freshly grated
$^1/_2$ teaspoon freshly grated nutmeg
300 g (11 oz) cooked ham,
   roughly chopped
400 g (14 oz) mozzarella, roughly
   diced
salt and freshly ground black
   pepper

TO SERVE
$^1/_2$ quantity Basic Tomato Sauce
   (page 64), warmed
1 quantity Béchamel Sauce
   (page 75), warmed

meat

POULTRY AND GAME

pork with marsala • porchetta • dora's meat loaf • beef stew with mushroom crostini • calves' liver with butter and sage • steak tagliata with rocket, parmesan and balsamic dressing • veal parcels stuffed with cheese in a wild mushroom sauce • devilled poussin • chicken with cinnamon and lemon • mustard-roast chicken with caramelized onions • guinea fowl with apricots, chestnuts, prunes and vin santo • roast pheasant and guinea fowl in terracotta • wild boar with chocolate • rack of lamb in red wine, onions and rosemary

meat, poultry and game

My goodness, they eat a lot of meat in Tuscany! The most popular is pork, and it's prepared in every possible way you can imagine. We even visited a festival of pork in Torrita di Siena. Here we were shown how you can eat most parts of the animal, and what you can't eat is used in another way – like fat for polishing shoes or making soap. Nothing is wasted and this applies to any animal. Italians were too poor, too recently, to be wasteful of natural resources and the habit has remained with them. So offal, cheek, brain are widely used and cheaper cuts of meat are popular for stewing.

The pig is the king of the table

I was vegetarian for two and a half years until I first went to Italy. That was 20 years ago but I don't think the country's meat-eating tradition has changed much. I was broke and hungry on a train with my friend William. The family opposite were enjoying their proscuitto-filled *panini*; thin slices of deliciously salty cured pork oozed out of the bread. They needed a bottle opener and I had one in my bag, so offered it to them. In turn they offered me a *panino*. William started to say that I was *vegetariana* but he would like one. I clapped one hand over his mouth and reached out with the other to grab my lunch! William was gobsmacked, I was satisfied and I proceeded to eat meat and enjoy it from then on.

Porchetta: pork and herbs

No market in Tuscany would be complete without a *porchetta* van. On the previous day a whole pig is boned, stuffed with a mixture of rosemary, sage and salt, and put on a metal pole. It is then sewn up and cooked in a special oven. The result is salty, crunchy crackling around succulent pork and herbs. The salt that falls away from the inside is served separately so that those with a yearning for salty things can add it to their meat. The pork is sliced and served cold in bread rolls. Giancarlo is so keen on it that he hired a *porchetta* van for our wedding and helped the owner cook the pig the day before. We and our guests were eating *porchetta* in *panini* at 11 o'clock on our wedding night!

Sausages: a Tuscan speciality

The classic, lean pork Tuscan sausages contain no bread, only a few herbs, some garlic and sometimes red wine. There are so many recipes for them: sausages *alla brace*, simply grilled; sausages in beans; sausages in *ragu* for pasta; crostini with sausagemeat. Tuscans split sausages and use the meat rather than buying sausagemeat. We tried this in the UK with British pork sausages but the meat is too finely ground to be used in the same way the Tuscans use it, so go for good-quality pork mince instead.

In our kitchen in the UK we use a meat grinder, something my mother always had clamped to the end of the table for grinding leftover meat to make rissoles. Giancarlo's mother made *polpettone* (meat loaf). Our children love stuffing meat into the top and winding the handle as I did when I was little – despite my mother's warning about turning my little fingers into sausages. We occasionally make sausages but the process takes ages and is quite fiddly. The best bet is to find a good butcher and buy the best sausages you can – they will be more filling because they contain more lean protein and less fat.

Beef and T-bone steaks

Huge white cattle – Chianina – are bred in the Val di Chiana, a valley between Chiusi and Arezzo in Tuscany. It is these animals that provide the celebrated Florentine T-bone steaks enjoyed by Tuscans. Prehistoric cave drawings indicate that meat from this breed were enjoyed by the early settlers in Tuscany, the Etruscans. The cattle may well be one of the oldest breeds in existence, and are now farmed in the United States and Canada because of their fast growth rate and heavy muscling. Chianina are known for their fine-textured meat, and the natural marbling of fat that runs through it adds a wonderful flavour to the beef.

If you can't find Chianina beef, choose Aberdeen Angus from a good butcher. It should have been hung, by the butcher, for a minimum of two weeks or a maximum of a month, to ensure it is succulent and tender. Steaks in Italy are usually cooked *alla brace* (see page 82) but failing this, grill or fry them. Always choose a steak with some marbled fat and a good fatty rind.

Cooking your steak as you like it

You can tell when a steak is cooked to your liking by comparing the feeling when you press the flesh under your thumb with what the steak in the frying pan feels like when you press it. For a rare steak, touch the top of your thumb with the top of the first finger on the same hand, and feel the flesh under your thumb with one of the fingers of your other hand. Then press the steak. For a medium rare, medium well done or well done steak, use your middle finger, ring finger or little finger respectively.

Veal: a popular Tuscan meat

Veal is almost as popular in Tuscany as pork. There are two types: *vitella di latte*, veal from a young calf that is still suckling; and *vitellone*, which comes from an animal aged 18–20 months. *Vitellone* has more flavour than *vitella* and its flesh is deep pink. Suckling calves have white flesh, which may look attractive but has less flavour.

Poultry and game

Though chicken is not as popular in Tuscany as it is in the UK the quality is excellent. The birds are full of flavour and usually corn-fed, which gives them an attractive golden-yellow colour. Older birds are sold to make stock – they are boiled whole for a minimum of 3 hours. In the UK you may be able to buy one from a good butcher or a farm shop. The boiled meat can be removed from the carcass and is delicious fried with olive oil, salt, sultanas and pine nuts.

Guinea fowl are plentiful in Tuscany and Giancarlo's mother bred them on the farm. The meat is similar to that of chicken, but has a stronger flavour. Partridge, quail and pheasant are also eaten, during the hunting season.

Hunting for game

Hunting is a huge pastime in Italy and hunters go out to shoot every Thursday and at weekends in autumn and winter, during the hunting season. Sometimes their expeditions are pointless – they kill small songbirds that they have no intention of eating. Other times it's serious, and they are after deer or wild boar. It can take a group of hunters almost all day to track and kill a single boar. As in Britain, Tuscans like to shoot and eat pheasant, partridge, quail and hares. Rabbits are killed all year round and are a regular addition to the Tuscan diet.

Alla brace: cooking over embers

Alla brace means 'on the grill' and throughout Italy is one of the most popular ways of cooking meat or fish. For years Giancarlo and I, like many others in Britain, cooked over a gas barbecue because we were fed up with lighting charcoal on a cold and windy summer's day. But I don't know why we bothered with either, and didn't just cook indoors. The flavour would have been the same. Surely the whole point of barbecuing is the taste imparted to the food by the burning embers of the wood it is cooked over? That is precisely what Tuscans appreciate.

Italians light fires in a back garden, a courtyard, a restaurant kitchen. They gather wood from nearby forests and cook over it. In Tuscany we mainly used oak, which has a high burning temperature and does not fall apart too quickly. To cook *alla brace*, you have to wait for charcoal to form in the fire and then scrape it forward and put a grill over it. The meat, fish or vegetables sit about 10 cm (4 in) above the embers and cook quickly. It is totally different to a gas barbecue, and so much more satisfying. On the course we made an evening of it twice a week. It was wonderful to sit around the fire with a glass of local wine and watch the flames. The children loved to wrap potatoes and onions in foil and throw them into the fire. After 10 minutes they were retrieved, piping hot, ready to be eaten, with butter for the potatoes and balsamic vinegar for the onions. At local fairs there were fires in braziers with grills fixed over them. And some of the restaurants had fires in their kitchens, built into the walls and with vast chimneys to carry away the smoke. I would love to see more *alla brace* cooking in the UK.

Everyone eats pork in Tuscany and Giancarlo's family were no exception in that they bred pigs. Whenever his father, Memmo, sold a litter of piglets to the butcher he received a piece of pork in part exchange. Giancarlo's mother, as the family cook, came up with a variety of ways of preparing their staple meat. Using vegetable or nut oil, instead of the more usual olive oil, means the delicate flavour of the pork isn't masked. The Marsala wine adds plenty of flavour. If you can't find it, replace it with a medium sherry.

pork with marsala

SERVES 4

600 g (1 lb 5 oz) pork fillet, sliced
   into 4 cm (1$\frac{1}{2}$ in) medallions
plain flour, for dredging
4 tablespoons sunflower oil
100 ml (3$\frac{1}{2}$ fl oz) Marsala wine
20 g ($\frac{3}{4}$ oz) butter
3–4 tablespoons Chicken Stock
   (page 44) or Beef Stock (page 45)
salt and freshly ground black
   pepper
Porcini and Pecorino Refried Mash
   (page 36), to serve

Flatten the pork medallions slightly with the back of a wooden spoon. Put the flour on a plate, season it with salt and pepper and coat the medallions in the seasoned flour.

Heat the oil in a frying pan until hot and fry the medallions over a medium heat for 10 minutes or until cooked, turning once halfway through cooking.

To see if the medallions are cooked, pierce one with a skewer or sharp knife. If the juices run clear it is ready. Drain the oil out of the pan, keeping back the medallions. Pour in the Marsala wine and reduce for a further 2 minutes with the heat still high.

Add the butter and stock and stir well. Remove the medallions, place on a warm serving dish and pour the juices over them. Serve with Porcini and Pecorino Refried Mash.

Franco Taruschio, who used to be chef/owner of the Walnut Tree Inn in Abergavenny, taught Marco Moscoloni, our sous-chef, how to make this dish. He's since made it his own by adding slices of salumi. Traditionally porchetta *is served cold, in a bread roll. It can also be thickly sliced and served as roast pork. Our version is finely sliced and served with a balsamic dressing as a starter.*

porchetta

SERVES 8–10 AS A STARTER OR 4–6 AS A MAIN COURSE

2 kg (4$\frac{1}{2}$ lb) belly of pork, ribs removed
handful of fresh sage
leaves from 5 sprigs fresh rosemary, chopped
4 garlic cloves, roughly chopped
10 slices *sopressata* (see page 20) or mortadella
extra-virgin olive oil, for brushing
salt and freshly ground black pepper
balsamic vinegar and extra-virgin olive oil, for drizzling (optional)

Preheat the oven to 220°C/425°F/Gas 7.

Lay the pork out flat and sprinkle with the herbs, garlic and seasoning. Place the *sopressata* or mortadella on top.

Roll the meat up like a Swiss roll. Push a butcher's needle or a skewer through the meat to make a hole, then thread a length of string through. (Cover the meat with a cloth to prevent the needle or skewer sticking into your hand when you push it through the skin.) Do this about seven times along the length of the roll, and try to close up the skin at either end.

Score the skin between the string, using a sharp knife. Brush the pork generously with olive oil, and place it on a rack in the oven. Cook for 10 minutes.

Reduce the temperature to 160°C/325°F/Gas 3. Half-fill a roasting tin with water and put it underneath the *porchetta*. This prevents the meat burning and gives it a crispy skin. Cover the top of the meat with damp greaseproof paper and cook for 1$\frac{1}{2}$ hours. Remove the paper 10 minutes before the end of the cooking time.

The meat is cooked when a skewer inserted into it comes out dry. If it comes out wet, it's not ready.

Either serve the *porchetta* warm, in thick slices, in *panini*, or leave it to cool and serve thinly sliced as a starter, drizzled with balsamic vinegar and olive oil.

Both my mother and Giancarlo's mother made meat loaf when we were children and we both loved it. This is the Tuscan version, polpettone, *as made by Dora, a tiny Sicilian woman who worked at the Hotel Le Rotelle. She may be from Sicily, but she has acquired an amazing knowledge of Tuscan cooking after living in Torrita di Siena for 30 years. She also grows wonderfully tasty vegetables, which she sells at the market, and which we lived off when we were in Tuscany.*

dora's meat loaf

SERVES 4

110 g (4$^1/_2$ oz) breadcrumbs,
  made from stale white bread
400 g (14 oz) minced beef
2 garlic cloves, finely chopped
25 g (1 oz) fresh parsley, chopped
75 g (3 oz) onion, chopped
40 g (1$^1/_2$ oz) carrot, chopped
100 g (4 oz) ham, sliced
plain flour, for coating
5 tablespoons olive oil
1 quantity Basic Tomato Sauce
  (page 64)
salt and freshly ground black
  pepper
Porcini and Pecorino Refried Mash
  (page 36), to serve

Mix the breadcrumbs with the mince, garlic, parsley, onion and carrot, and season with salt and pepper. Form into a log shape, then hollow out a narrow trough along the centre. Roll up the ham slices and push them into the trough. Push the mince back over the ham to form a log again. Coat the meat loaf with flour.

Heat the olive oil in a frying pan, then place the meat loaf in the pan. Brown on all sides over a medium heat – this will take 10–15 minutes. Be careful not to break the loaf up as you turn it.

Make sure the tomato sauce is simmering. It's important that it is not too thick – add a little more stock if it is. Carefully place the meat loaf in a large saucepan and pour the tomato sauce over it. Cook over a medium heat for 45 minutes–1 hour. If it starts to stick on the bottom of the pan, turn the heat down.

To see if the meatloaf is cooked, insert a knife into the centre. If the juices run clear, it's ready. Serve with Porcini and Pecorino Refried Mash.

Giancarlo cooked this stew in Tuscany when we were having a party. It takes a long time and can't be hurried, but it's well worth it. It's great for dinner parties because, once cooked, it can be kept warm in a low oven until you are ready to eat. We serve it with Mushroom Crostini (page 33).

beef stew with mushroom crostini

SERVES 6–8

1 quantity *soffritto* ingredients
  (page 46 or 48)
1.25 kg (2½ lb) stewing beef, cut
  into bite-sized cubes
200 ml (7 fl oz) red wine
1 kg (2¼ lb) plum tomatoes,
  chopped
300 ml (½ pint) Beef Stock
  (page 45), plus extra if necessary
1 tablespoon tomato purée
800 g (1¾ lb) potatoes
salt and freshly ground black
  pepper

TO SERVE
Mushroom Crostini (page 33)
Sformato of Carrots (page 34)
roast vegetables and mashed
  potatoes

Cook the *soffritto* as on page 46 or 48. Once it's ready, add the meat and fry, stirring constantly, over a medium heat until browned. This will get rid of any excess liquid from the meat.

Add the wine and cook for 2 minutes to reduce. Add the tomatoes, stock, tomato purée and seasoning, then simmer, uncovered, over a low heat for 2½–3 hours.

Check the stew from time to time, and, if necessary, top it up with more stock to prevent it drying out.

Cut the potatoes into 2.5 cm (1 in) chunks and add them to the stew 40 minutes before the end of cooking time. Top the stew with Mushroom Crostini, and serve Sformato of Carrots, roast vegetables and mashed potatoes on the side.

A traditional Tuscan dish, this combines calves' liver and fresh sage and was one of Giancarlo's father's favourites. It is very quick and easy to prepare, and is great served with Luciano's Roast Potatoes (page 37) or Porcini and Pecorino Refried Mash (page 36). It is best to use a non-stick frying pan – make sure it and the oil are hot, but not smoking hot, to avoid overcooking the liver. This dish is usually on the menu at one of our restaurants.

calves' liver with butter and sage

SERVES 2

plain flour, for dredging
2 pieces calves' liver, each
   weighing about 100 g (4 oz)
4 tablespoons olive oil
2 garlic cloves
65 g (2$\frac{1}{2}$ oz) butter
8 fresh sage leaves
salt and freshly ground black
   pepper

Mix the flour, salt and pepper together on a plate. Press each piece of liver into the flour, then turn it over and repeat on the other side, until fully coated.

Heat the olive oil in a non-stick frying pan and fry the garlic over a medium heat for 1 minute.

Increase the heat to high and add the liver to the pan. Fry for 30 seconds on each side for medium-cooked liver, about 45 seconds on each side for well done.

Turn the heat down, pour away the oil and add the butter and sage leaves to the pan. Cook the liver until the butter has melted and serve immediately, dressed with the butter, sage and garlic.

This steak has an amazing flavour when it is cooked alla brace, *over hot embers. However, it also works well on a griddle or in a frying pan. It's a great quick supper or lunch, and we always have it on the bar menu at the Caffé Caldesi.* Tagliata *means sliced, and this is how the steak is served. Buy the best quality, most syrupy balsamic vinegar you can afford and drizzle it on sparingly at the end.*

steak tagliata
with rocket, parmesan and balsamic dressing

SERVES 1

250 g (9 oz) sirloin steak
2 tablespoons extra-virgin olive oil
40 g (1½ oz) rocket leaves
salt and freshly ground black
 pepper
balsamic vinegar, to drizzle
20 g (¾ oz) Parmesan, freshly
 shaved

Leave the fat on the steak, but make little cuts along the length of the rind. This will stop the meat shrinking as it cooks and keep it cooking evenly. Salt the steak well on both sides.

Heat the olive oil on a large griddle or in a frying pan until very hot. Cook the steak for 2–4 minutes on each side, according to how you like it (see page 81).

Meanwhile, arrange the rocket leaves on a serving plate.

When the steak is cooked to your liking, remove it from the pan and immediately cut it into slices 2 cm (1 in) thick.

Lay the slices on the rocket, keeping the steak as close to its original shape as possible. Drizzle over the vinegar, sprinkle with pepper and scatter with the Parmesan. Serve straight away.

These delicious little veal parcels are nearly always on the menu in our restaurants in the autumn, when wild mushrooms come into season. Tender slices of meat are wrapped around young pecorino. If you can't get this use another medium-hard cheese that will melt easily – try mozzarella or scarmorza.

veal parcels stuffed with cheese
in a wild mushroom sauce

SERVES 4

600 g (1 lb 5 oz) veal topside

250 g (9 oz) young pecorino, freshly grated

plain flour, for dredging

3–4 tablespoons olive oil

3–4 tablespoons white wine (not too sweet)

350 g (12 oz) wild mushrooms, sliced

1 sprig fresh rosemary

2 garlic cloves, crushed

100 ml (3$\frac{1}{2}$ fl oz) Chicken Stock (page 44)

salt and freshly ground black pepper

Luciano's Roast Potatoes (page 37), to serve

Cut the veal into eight slices, cover each slice with cling film and bash it with a rolling pin to form 15 × 13 cm (6 × 5 in) pieces. Don't be too rough or the meat will break up.

Divide the pecorino into eight portions and place one portion slightly off-centre on each slice of veal. Fold the veal over, cover with cling film and bash the sides gently to seal them. Season the parcels with salt and pepper.

Place the flour in a shallow bowl. Dip each parcel in the flour, turning once, so that each side is coated lightly.

Heat 2 tablespoons of the olive oil in a large frying pan and fry the parcels over a medium heat until browned on both sides.

Pour away the oil. Add the wine to the pan and heat for 1–2 minutes until it has evaporated completely.

Heat the remaining oil in another frying pan, add the mushrooms and fry until they are golden brown and slightly crispy. Season with salt and pepper, and add the rosemary and garlic.

Add the veal parcels to the mushroom mixture. Pour in the stock and bring to the boil. Cook for about 2 minutes to reduce. Remove the rosemary and garlic, and serve with Luciano's Roast Poatoes.

I love this combination of spicy chicken with rocket and Parmesan salad. It always feels very healthy and light to eat. We use our fingers to get the last remaining pieces of chicken off the bones. Make sure the poussin are well cooked, so that the skins are crispy.

devilled poussin

SERVES 2

2 poussin (baby chickens), weighing about 600–800 g (1 lb 5 oz–1³/₄ lb)
6 garlic cloves, 4 crushed with a knife and 2 finely chopped
4 sprigs fresh rosemary
5 tablespoons extra-virgin olive oil
2 fresh red chillies, seeded and finely chopped
salt and freshly ground black pepper
rocket leaves, Parmesan shavings and ¹/₂ lemon, halved, to serve

Preheat the oven to 200°C/400°F/Gas 6.

Place each poussin on its back and cut between the legs but not through to the backbone. Lay it out flat, remove any excess fat and pull out any remaining feathers. Cut off the parson's nose and the last section of the wings. Turn the poussin over and trim away any pieces in the cavity. Wash away any blood.

Season both sides of each poussin with salt and pepper and place on a baking tray. Put 2 crushed garlic cloves and 2 sprigs of rosemary under each bird.

Drizzle with the olive oil and roast for about 30–40 minutes (turn over halfway through cooking), until the juices run clear when a skewer is inserted into the birds.

Remove from the oven and sprinkle the poussin with the chillies and chopped garlic. Cook for a further 10 minutes.

Transfer to warm serving plates and serve each poussin with rocket leaves, Parmesan shavings and a lemon wedge for squeezing.

The wonderful medieval feel of this dish dates back to the days when spices were used in cooking to display a family's wealth. The spice trade that passed through Venice brought many delights from the Far East, and some have been part of Italian cooking ever since. In this recipe cinnamon combines with lemon to give the chicken a subtle tangy flavour.

chicken with cinnamon and lemon

SERVES 4

2 lemons
1 quantity Giancarlo's Soffritto
  (page 46)
plain flour, for dredging
1 × 1.5–2 kg (3¼ – 4½ lb)
  free-range chicken, jointed, or
  8 chicken pieces on the bone
5–6 tablespoons extra-virgin
  olive oil
100 ml (3½ fl oz) white wine
4 cinnamon sticks
200 ml (7 fl oz) Chicken Stock
  (page 44)
1 egg yolk
salt and freshly ground black
  pepper

TO SERVE
Sformato of Carrots (page 34)
Luciano's Roast Potatoes (page 37),
  mashed potatoes or rice

Peel the zest of one of the lemons into four long pieces, ensuring you have just the yellow and not the white pith. Squeeze the juice from both the lemons and set aside.

Cook the *soffritto* as on page 46. In the last few minutes of cooking time add the lemon zest.

Mix the flour, salt and pepper in a shallow bowl. Dip the chicken pieces into the flour and coat thoroughly. Heat the olive oil in a large pan and fry the chicken pieces over a medium heat until golden brown on all sides. Add the wine and cook for 5 minutes to reduce.

Add the *soffritto*, half the lemon juice and the cinnamon to the pan and stir well.

Add the stock, cover and cook over a low heat for about 30 minutes. Remove the lid and cook for a further 15 minutes or until the sauce has reduced and the chicken is cooked. Remove any large pieces of lemon zest and the cinnamon sticks.

Beat together the remaining lemon juice and the egg yolk in a small bowl. Remove the chicken from the heat and add the lemon and egg mixture a little at a time, stirring continuously to avoid it curdling. Serve immediately with Sformato of Carrots and Luciano's Roast Potaotes, mashed potatoes or rice. Do not reheat the chicken once you have added the lemon and egg mixture as it will mar the taste.

The Tuscan version of this dish uses rabbit, but as it's such an adaptable recipe, we usually make it with a whole chicken or with chicken joints instead. If you're going for the latter option, allow slightly less cooking time as the joints tend to cook faster than a whole bird. Italians use the strongest mustard they can find for this dish, but a strong English one will work just as well.

mustard-roast chicken
with caramelized onions

SERVES 4–6

1 kg (2¼ lb) onions, finely sliced
4 garlic cloves, halved and lightly crushed
1 × 170 g jar mustard
1 × 1.5 kg (3¼ lb) free-range chicken
5 tablespoons extra-virgin olive oil
5 tablespoons Chicken Stock (page 44)
125 ml (4½ fl oz) white wine
sea salt and freshly ground black pepper
Luciano's Roast Potoates (page 37), to serve

Preheat the oven to 180°C/350°F/Gas 4.

Place the sliced onions and garlic in an ovenproof dish, large enough to accomodate the chicken. Season with sea salt and pepper.

Spread the mustard over the skin of the chicken to coat thoroughly. Don't be worried about using too much mustard – it's absorbed by the chicken during the cooking and the sweet taste of the onions balances the flavours well. Place the chicken on top of the onions and season with more sea salt and pepper. Drizzle the olive oil over the chicken, place it in the oven and cook for 35 minutes until the skin is slightly crispy.

Turn the chicken over, pour the white wine over the chicken and the onions and cook for another 25 minutes. Turn the bird once more, then cook for a further 10 minutes to ensure the skin is golden and crispy. Add the stock when necessary, to stop the onions drying out.

To check if the meat is cooked, pierce a chicken leg with a skewer – when the juices run clear it is ready. Remove from the oven. Spoon some of the caramelized onions on to a warm plate, top with a portion of the chicken and serve with Luciano's Roast Potatoes.

This recipe has its origins in la cucina nobile – *the cooking of the nobility. It is a dish unlike most Tuscan recipes as it uses expensive ingredients, such as* vin santo, *and dried fruits. It is ideal for celebrations, or for warming autumnal or winter dinner parties.*

guinea fowl
with apricots, chestnuts, prunes and vin santo

SERVES 2

1 guinea fowl
50 g (2 oz) plain flour, sifted
100 ml (3$^{1}/_{2}$ fl oz) extra-virgin
   olive oil
1 quantity *soffritto* ingredients
   (page 46 or 48)
500 ml (18 fl oz) Chicken Stock
   (page 44), plus extra if necessary
16 dried prunes, stoned
16 dried apricots, stoned
16 whole chestnuts, about 120 g
   (4$^{1}/_{2}$ oz), roasted and peeled –
   tinned or vacuum-packed
   are fine
5–6 tablespoons *vin santo*
salt and freshly ground black
   pepper

Preheat the oven to 200°C/400°F/Gas 6.

Using a sharp knife, joint the guinea fowl into eight pieces. Season with salt and pepper. Place the flour on a plate and dip each piece of meat in to coat thoroughly on both sides. Shake off any excess.

Heat the olive oil in a large, non-stick, ovenproof frying pan. When hot, add the guinea fowl and cook over a medium heat for about 12 minutes, turning, until golden brown and crispy. Drain quickly on kitchen paper and set aside.

Clean the pan and cook the *soffritto* as on page 46 or 48.

Add the guinea fowl, stock, dried prunes, apricots, chestnuts and *vin santo* to the *soffritto* once it's ready. Stir to combine all the ingredients. Place the pan in the preheated oven and cook for about 40 minutes. Stir from time to time to ensure the fruits are covered by liquid. If, towards the end of the cooking time, it begins to look dry, add a little more stock.

To check if the meat is cooked, pierce the guinea fowl with a skewer – when the juices run clear it is ready. Remove from the oven. Divide the meat and fruit between four plates so that everyone gets two portions of guinea fowl, four apricots and four chestnuts. Pour the juice from the pan over and serve immediately.

This versatile dish can be changed to suit whatever game or poultry is available. You can also alter the vegetables to suit the season. Although not available in Tuscany, sweet potatoes are a delicious alternative to the usual kind, but remove the carrots if you use them, or the dish will be too sweet. It is cooked in one pot – terracotta, if possible, as this improves the flavour. Serve straight to the table if you have an attractive pot. If not, use a roasting tin for the cooking and transfer the dish to a serving plate.

roast pheasant and guinea fowl
in terracotta

SERVES 6

10 fresh sage leaves, finely
   chopped
leaves from 2 sprigs fresh
   rosemary, finely chopped
1 garlic head, split into cloves and
   chopped
1 guinea fowl, halved
1 pheasant, halved
3 carrots, cut into 2.5 cm (1 in)
   chunks
2 courgettes, cut into 2.5 cm (1 in)
   chunks
2 potatoes, peeled and cut into
   4 cm (1$\frac{1}{2}$ in) chunks
100 ml (3$\frac{1}{2}$ fl oz) extra-virgin
   olive oil
salt and freshly ground black
   pepper

Preheat the oven to 200°C/400°F/Gas 6.

Combine the sage, rosemary and garlic with salt and pepper and mix well. Make several 2.5 cm (1 in) cuts in the birds and stuff the herb mixture into the cuts.

Put the vegetables into a large terracotta pot and pour over half the olive oil. Mix and season well. Lay the birds on top and drizzle with the remaining oil. Roast in the oven for 30–40 minutes. After 15 minutes, baste the birds with the cooking juices and turn them over.

To check if the meat is cooked, pierce each bird with a skewer – when the juices run clear it is ready. Remove the birds from the pot and cut each one into eight portions. Replace on top of the vegetables and return to the oven for 5 minutes.

Remove from the oven and leave to rest for 20 minutes before serving. This relaxes the meat, letting it become more tender. Serve with the potatoes and vegetables from the pot.

Cinghiale (wild boar) was only served to the nobility in Giancarlo's youth, but is now popular everywhere in Tuscany. For some years his mother worked for a wealthy family in Montepulciano and he remembers tasting delicious wild boar stews at their house. Remember to plan ahead as the boar needs to be marinated overnight. If you can't get wild boar, try venison.

wild boar with chocolate

SERVES 6

200 g (7 oz) onions
100 g (4 oz) carrots
150 g (5 oz) celery
1.25 kg (2½ lb) wild boar
2 bay leaves
6 juniper berries
1–1.5 litres (1¾–2½ pints) robust red wine
5 tablespoons olive oil
1 sprig fresh rosemary, finely chopped
1 sprig fresh thyme, finely chopped
550 ml (18 fl oz) Beef Stock (page 45)
85 ml (3 fl oz) red wine vinegar
90 g (3¼ oz) cocoa
75 g (3 oz) raisins
50 g (2 oz) pine nuts
salt and freshly ground black pepper
mashed potatoes and spinach, to serve

Roughly chop the onions and cut the carrots and celery into large chunks. Cut the boar into bite-sized cubes. Place the boar, onions, carrots, celery, bay leaves and juniper berries in a shallow, non-metallic dish and pour in enough red wine to cover. Leave overnight in the fridge to marinate.

Drain the liquid from the meat and vegetables and discard. Chop the vegetables finely.

Heat the olive oil in a large flameproof casserole dish or pan and add the chopped vegetables. Add the rosemary and thyme, and season with salt and pepper. Fry for about 15 minutes over a medium heat, until the vegetables have softened.

Spread the meat on a chopping board or large plate and season with salt and pepper. Add to the casserole dish or pan and fry, uncovered, for 15 minutes, stirring frequently. Add 300 ml (½ pint) of red wine and the stock. Simmer over a low heat, uncovered, for 1½–2 hours or until the meat is tender and cooked.

Remove the meat using a slotted spoon and set aside in a warm place, covered, while you make the sauce. Skim off most of the excess oil with a spoon. Add the vinegar, cocoa, raisins and pine nuts. Stir, and cook for 10 minutes.

Return the boar to the pan and stir well. Serve with mashed potatoes and spinach.

Giancarlo teaches this dish on our course. He says it reminds him of a recipe his Aunt Pasquina cooked every Easter when the spring lambs were born – and Giancarlo loves re-creating dishes from his childhood. Lamb is not as popular in Tuscany as it is in Britain, but lots of sheep are reared in the hills around Pienza to produce pecorino.

rack of lamb in red wine, onions and rosemary

SERVES 2

1 rack of lamb
3 tablespoons olive oil
5 shallots
2 garlic cloves, crushed
2 sprigs fresh thyme
1 large sprig fresh rosemary
200 g (7 oz) wild mushrooms
200 ml (7 fl oz) red wine
salt and freshly ground black
   pepper
Cannellini Bean and Rosemary
   Mash (page 36) and early spring
   greens, to serve

Preheat the oven to 190°C/375°F/Gas 5.

Cut away most of the fat from the top of the rack of lamb and trim away the fascia (the sheath that holds in the muscle). Trim between the bones.

Heat 2 tablespoons olive oil in a frying pan and add the shallots. Fry over a low heat for about 10 minutes or until they start to soften. Add the garlic, thyme, rosemary and mushrooms. Continue frying for a few minutes, then add 150 ml (5 fl oz) of the wine.

Meanwhile, season the lamb on all sides with salt and pepper. Heat the remaining oil in a separate frying pan. When hot, fry the lamb until it is seared on all sides, including the ends. Add the remaining wine to the pan to deglaze it. Let the wine reduce for 2 minutes. Transfer the lamb to an ovenproof dish and spread the mushroom mixture around the meat.

Bake for 25–35 minutes. Serve straight away with Cannellini Bean and Rosemary Mash and early spring greens.

fish

AND SEAFOOD

grilled fish with parsley, lemon and chilli dressing • perch with tomatoes, capers and black olives • pan-fried sea bass with garlic and cherry tomatoes • monkfish cooked with parsley and white wine • oven-baked sea bream with tuscan herb stuffing • livia's baccalà • steamed mussels • warm octopus, potato and lemon salad

fish and seafood

When creating the fish lesson for our course, I asked Giancarlo what we should emphasize about the Italian way of cooking fish. His answer was, 'Nothing. You don't have to do anything to fish.' Not much help when we had a group of students about to arrive! However, it did sum up how Tuscans treat fish. They grill it, fry it, maybe throw a few herbs at it, but that's it. The flavour is so delicate, why mask it with anything else? And what's better than locally caught fish simply cooked and full of flavour?

Giancarlo loves to stuff a whole fish with local herbs – it is easy to do and always delights. The fish can be cooked on the grill or, as on page 112, it can be baked in the oven (in foil or paper parcels, if you wish). It is always popular when we teach it on our course.

Where to buy fresh fish
Giancarlo was amazed by the variety of fish available at Mr Fish's Shop (it really is called that!) in Torrita di Siena, a small town near our school. In his childhood, fish was rare and was provided by a man on a bike who brought eels or lake fish to his house. Occasionally, someone from his family went fishing or caught eels by hand, wearing hessian gloves and frantically chasing them through the long grasses as they tried to escape. The only fish available at the market were salt cod and canned salted sardines, tuna or anchovies. Nowadays, there are often two vans selling just fish, brought from the coast of Tuscany or caught in the local lakes.

Fish start to deteriorate as soon as they are caught and killed, so try to buy fresh ones that haven't travelled far, or fish or shellfish that have been frozen on the boat. Find a good fishmonger if you can – the shop will always be busy and this ensures a frequent turnover of produce. Or buy from a good fresh fish counter at a supermarket. If you are lucky enough to live near the sea, find out if, where and when you can buy fish direct from a fisherman.

How to tell if fish is fresh
A fish's eyes should be clear, not opaque, and not sunken into the surrounding flesh. The scales should be firmly attached, unless the fish has been descaled. It should smell fresh and like the sea or, if it is from a lake or river, it may have an earthy smell. The gills should be bright red. If they feel sticky or there is an unpleasant odour the fish is past its best – the gills are one of the first places to look for signs of decomposition. The flesh should be firm and spring back when touched.

Either buy fish with their heads and tails or, if you prefer, ask the fishmonger to fillet them for you, and keep the bones for fish stock. If you need extra ingredients for stock ask for a head or a rack (fish skeleton).

If you're buying fillets or steaks you won't be able to look at the eyes or gills, but you can smell the flesh and look at it. It should be flexible and not starting to separate. Red spots on a white-fish fillet could indicate bruising. For more information on fish of all types, including how to clean, scale and fillet, try www.passionate aboutfish.co.uk.

Storing and preparing shellfish

Mussels and clams should always be bought live and can be stored in a cool place, covered with wet newspaper, for up to two days. A cool garage is suitable for this, or the warmest shelf in your fridge. Like fish, they should have a sea-fresh smell.

When buying shellfish, check that the shells are tightly closed or close rapidly when tapped – this indicates they are alive. Any mussels with broken shells should be thrown away. Although it is usually unnecessary to clean or purge shellfish, you can get rid of any grit by immersing them overnight in 100 ml (3^{1}/$_{2}$ fl oz) water with ^{1}/$_{2}$ teaspoon of salt added. They will open and close in this as it is similar to sea water and the grit will be washed out.

Most fresh mussels and clams come ready prepared, but once purchased they should be

washed and scrubbed to remove any remaining dirt and beards. Once cooked, discard any unopened ones.

Avoid buying prawns or langoustines with patches of black on their tails. This may indicate the presence of melanosis, which will not harm humans but will make the shellfish turn black when cooked. It is often best to buy frozen shellfish as they are usually frozen directly after being caught. When choosing them, check for white patches on the shells – this is freezer burn and will spoil the texture of the flesh.

Sea fish

Italy's long coastline means that fish has always been popular for those living near the sea. However, people living in inland Italy had to cook with river and lake fish, such as pike, trout and freshwater bream. Salted and dried fish became popular and a wealth of recipes were invented in order to use *baccalà*, salt cod. Larger private estates maintained their own fish ponds, but those who were less well off relied on fishmongers in the towns and travelling vans in the countryside.

Tuscany's lake and river fish

Lake fish are popular in Tuscany as Italians like to use local produce. The Hotel Le Rotelle is far from the coast but close to three lakes. The flesh of freshwater fish tastes earthy and slightly muddy, and is a bit sweeter than that of sea fish. A restaurant we go to regularly, Da Gino's on the edge of Lake Chiusi, serves mostly lake fish such as carp or perch.

Giancarlo remembers eating *coregone*, a lake fish similar to sea bass, at Lake Bolsena when he was 16. Tuscans like this wonderful fish oven-roasted. *Coregone* was so special that people travelled from miles away to eat it. Lake Bolsena is in the caldera of a dormant volcano so the water is deep and cold, which makes *coregone* flesh very firm, and able to withstand cooking without falling apart.

Italians normally ate fish on a Friday, following the Church's precepts. The Church deemed that good Christians should eat fish on Fridays and fast days because it was thought that, as fish are cold blooded, they would help cool the body and soul, and therefore encourage reflection and spirituality. Meat in contrast would heat the body and induce passion.

How to enhance flavours naturally

I am sometimes disappointed by the lack of flavour in plain cooked fish or shellfish. In a restaurant in Sardinia I ate fish that had an amazingly strong flavour. I asked the chef how he achieved it and he pointed to an open fire outside the window. He also let me in on his secret, which was to spread a very thin coating of *bottarga* (tuna roe) over the fish and shellfish before it was cooked. You have to be very sparing with this, as it can be overpowering. But a small amount can give slightly bland fish a wonderful flavour.

The other popular natural flavour-enhancer is salt. In Tuscany we used salt from the salt pans of Trapani in Sicily. Its taste has no trace of bitterness and marries perfectly with fish. Use a solution of 100 ml (3$\frac{1}{2}$ fl oz) water with $\frac{1}{2}$ teaspoon of salt added to 'brine' prawns. Leave them in it for 40 minutes before cooking and they will have a lot more flavour. They don't have to be live – you can even brine frozen peeled prawns.

This fresh-tasting, uncomplicated dish sums up the Italians' attitude to fish – keep it simple and bring out the flavours. Most fish can be cooked in the way described below, so have fun experimenting and don't feel you have to stick to the varieties we've listed below. This is also a great way of cooking fish alla brace (see page 82). The dressing is very fresh, and the chilli provides quite a kick, so add a little less if you want a milder heat. The fish should be served straight away once it's cooked, but the dressing can be made up to two hours in advance.

grilled fish with parsley, lemon and chilli dressing

SERVES 4

200 g (7 oz) cod fillet
200 g (7 oz) salmon fillet
200 g (7 oz) squid, cleaned and scored
200 g (7 oz) sea bass fillet
8 king prawns, shells on
2 tablespoons olive oil
salt and freshly ground black pepper
rocket leaves, to serve
1 lemon, cut into quarters, to serve

FOR THE DRESSING
15 g ($^1/_2$ oz) parsley, roughly torn
finely grated zest of $^1/_2$ lemon
1 garlic clove
1 medium red chilli, finely chopped
100 ml ($3^1/_2$ fl oz) extra-virgin olive oil

Preheat the grill to its highest setting.

Season the fish all over with salt and pepper. Lay the fish directly onto the grill pan, without the rack, or onto some kitchen foil. Brush with 1 tablespoon olive oil and put under the grill, close to the heat for 10–15 minutes.

Meanwhile, make the dressing by combining all the ingredients. Season to taste.

Turn the fish and baste with the remaining olive oil. Leave under the grill for a further 10 minutes, or until the fish is cooked through.

Place the fish on a bed of rocket leaves. Drizzle with the parsley, lemon and chilli dressing and serve with a lemon wedge on each plate.

Our students, and our children, loved the wonderful array of local fish and shellfish in Mr Fish's Shop – our fishmonger in Torrita di Siena. For this recipe, try to find little salted capers in a jar rather than the ones preserved in brine, which never lose their vinegary flavour. And choose the shrivelled black olives sold loose by delis. Ask to taste one before buying – if you like it raw you will like it in the dish. Canned olives are usually too overpowering. If you can't get perch, use any white fish, such as cod, pollock or haddock.

perch with tomatoes, capers and black olives

SERVES 4

plain flour, for dredging
4 perch fillets, each weighing
   about 250 g (9 oz)
5 tablespoons olive oil
1 quantity Basic Tomato Sauce
   (page 64)
100 g (4 oz) salted capers,
   thoroughly rinsed
100 g (4 oz) black olives
200 ml (7 fl oz) Fish Stock (page 43)
   or Vegetable Stock (page 43),
   as necessary
salt and freshly ground black
   pepper
fresh parsley, torn, to garnish
crusty bread, to serve

Mix the flour, salt and pepper together on a plate, then dredge the perch fillets.

Heat the olive oil in a frying pan, add the fillets and fry over a medium heat until golden.

Warm the tomato sauce in a large pan and place the fillets gently in the sauce.

Add the capers and olives and cook, uncovered, over a low heat for 15 minutes.

If the contents of the pan begin to dry out, add a little stock.

Garnish with parsley and serve with plenty of crusty bread.

It's easy to get sea bass both in the UK and in Italy. This method of cooking perfectly illustrates the Italian attitude to fish and is another favourite dish from our restaurant. The juice from the fish, the cherry tomatoes and the garlic makes a simple sauce for the fish.

pan-fried sea bass with garlic and cherry tomatoes

SERVES 4

flour, for dredging
4 sea bass fillets
2 tablespoons extra-virgin olive oil
4 garlic cloves, skins left on but
   crushed
12 cherry tomatoes
3 tablespoons white wine
sea salt and freshly ground black
   pepper
sautéed spinach, to serve

Mix the flour with the salt and pepper in a shallow bowl. Coat each sea bass fillet with flour and set aside.

Heat the oil in a frying pan and place the fish in the pan, skin side down. Add the garlic and cook for 5 minutes, until you see the fish beginning to cook.

Turn the fish over and add the tomatoes. Cook for another 2 minutes, being very careful not to overcook the fish or it will become dry.

Pour off the excess oil and add the white wine. Cook for about 1 minute to reduce. Make sure the fish is cooked through.

Serve the fish with sautéed spinach, drizzled with the juices from the pan. Give each person three cherry tomatoes and a garlic clove.

This is one of Giancarlo's favourite ways to cook monkfish.

It is quick and simple and, apart from the fish, is made from

ingredients we always have in the house.

monkfish cooked with parsley and white wine

SERVES 4

200 g (7 oz) plain flour

600 g (1 lb 5 oz) monkfish, cut into 4 cm (1$\frac{1}{2}$ in) cubes

3–4 tablespoons olive oil

100 ml (3$\frac{1}{2}$ fl oz) white wine

100 g (4 oz) butter

100 ml (3$\frac{1}{2}$ fl oz) Fish Stock (page 43)

20 g ($\frac{3}{4}$ oz) fresh parsley, roughly chopped

salt and freshly ground black pepper

Cannellini Bean and Rosemary Mash (page 36) and steamed broccoli, to serve

Put the flour into a bowl with the salt and pepper, and mix well. Roll the monkfish cubes in the mixture.

Heat the olive oil in a frying pan until a piece of fish sizzles instantly when added. Cook the fish until it is golden on all sides.

Pour away the excess oil and add the wine. Cook over a medium heat for a couple of minutes to reduce, then add the butter and stock. Reduce again for a couple of minutes, then add the parsley. Cook for 1 minute, just to soften the parsley, and serve immediately with Cannellini Bean and Rosemary Mash and steamed broccoli.

We use this recipe on our courses all the time. It is easy and has never failed us. For the children, I use a fillet of white fish or salmon, with fewer herbs and salt, and cook the fish in cartoccio (see below), with the herbs tucked underneath.

oven-baked sea bream with tuscan herb stuffing

SERVES 4

4 sea bream, cleaned and
   descaled
5 tablespoons extra-virgin olive oil
Luciano's Roast Potatoes (page 37),
   to serve

FOR THE STUFFING
6 fresh sage leaves
4 sprigs fresh thyme
4 sprigs fresh parsley
4 garlic cloves, skins left on but
   crushed
sea salt and freshly ground black
   pepper
2 fresh red chillies, seeded and
   roughly chopped (optional)

Preheat the oven to 180°C/350°F/Gas 4. Brush a baking sheet with a little of the olive oil.

Hold one of the fish open with one hand, and with the other hand put one-quarter of the stuffing ingredients into the cavity. Repeat with the remaining fish and stuffing ingredients.

Place the fish on the greased baking sheet and drizzle over the remaining oil. Bake for 20–25 minutes until cooked through, depending on the size of the fish.

Alternatively, the fish can be cooked *in cartoccio* – in individual foil or greaseproof paper parcels. This steams rather than bakes them and concentrates the flavours more. Place each fish on a piece of foil or greaseproof paper large enough to wrap it in and bring the two shorter edges together. Fold them together with a little pleat pointing down towards the fish. Then fold each long edge in the same way. This forms a sealed parcel and the juices should not be able to escape. Place the parcels in a roasting tin and bake as above. The fish can be served in the foil or paper.

Whichever method you use, place the fish on warm plates and serve with generous helpings of Luciano's Roast Potatoes.

When Giancarlo was growing up in inland Tuscany the main fish eaten was baccalà *(salt cod) – it was available all year round, and easily transported to markets or by fish-sellers on bicycles. One of Livia's specialities is her* baccalà *with tomatoes and onions. You need to plan ahead if you want to make this dish – the cod has to be soaked in water for two days. Look for* baccalà *in Italian or Portuguese delis.*

livia's baccalà

SERVES 6

1 *baccalà* (salt cod), weighing about 1 kg (2¼ lb)
plain flour, for dredging
150 ml (½ pint) olive oil
1 large onion, sliced into 1 cm (½ in) rings
500 g (1 lb 2 oz) ripe tomatoes, peeled
1 fresh red chilli, seeded and finely chopped
100 ml (3½ fl oz) Fish Stock (page 43), as necessary
small bunch of fresh parsley, roughly chopped
freshly ground black pepper
crusty white bread, to serve

Soak the cod in water for two days. Change the water twice a day to wash off the excess salt.

Take the cod out of the water, cut off the fins and cut it in to large chunks.

Put the flour on a plate and roll the pieces of cod in it to coat them lightly.

Heat 4 tablespoons of the olive oil in a frying pan and fry the onion rings over a medium heat for about 10 minutes until softened.

Heat the remaining oil in a separate pan and fry the cod pieces on both sides until golden brown, to seal them.

Add the tomatoes and chilli to the onion in the frying pan and season with pepper. When the cod is golden brown, add it to this tomato sauce and cook over a low heat for 30 minutes. Add a little stock, if necessary, to stop the sauce becoming dry. Be gentle with the fish as it can easily flake.

Stir in the fresh parsley and heat through.

Serve on warm plates, accompanied by crusty bread.

We couldn't resist buying bags of live mussels from Mr Fish's Shop in Torrita di Siena. They are so quick to cook and this dish, which is one of our favourites, is great for lunch or supper.

steamed mussels

SERVES 4

1 kg (2¼ lb) live mussels, scrubbed and beards removed (see pages 105–6)
5 tablespoons olive oil
3 garlic cloves, lightly crushed
1 fresh red chilli, seeded and chopped
100 ml (3½ fl oz) white wine (not too sweet)
25 g (1 oz) butter
crusty white bread, to serve

Put the mussels in a large pan. Add the olive oil, garlic and chilli, cover and cook over a medium heat for 5 minutes.

Add the wine and butter and cook for a further 5 minutes. Discard any mussels that do not open.

Serve in warm bowls, with crusty white bread to mop up the juices. Don't forget a spare bowl to put the shells in.

A few years ago we stayed in San Remo on the north-west coast of Italy where the very excited owner of a restaurant we visited told us Luciano Pavarotti had eaten his speciality dish – octopus salad – the week before. He urged us to try it. Octopus is probably not what I would have chosen from the menu, but if it's good enough for Luciano, I thought, it will be good enough for me. It was wonderful, served tiepido *(tepid) to bring out the flavours of the octopus, lemon, potatoes and parsley. No one flavour overshadowed another and the salad was dressed in delicious Ligurian extra-virgin olive oil. Giancarlo was keen to re-create it for me back home and this is the result.*

warm octopus, potato and lemon salad

SERVES 6

1 kg (2¼ lb) octopus
1 carrot
½ onion
1 celery stick
2 bay leaves
4 medium potatoes, unpeeled
1 tablespoon lemon juice
5 tablespoons extra-virgin olive oil
small bunch of fresh parsley, roughly chopped
1 fresh red chilli, seeded and finely chopped
sea salt and freshly ground black pepper
crusty white bread, to serve

Put the octopus in plenty of cold water and bring to the boil. Add the carrot, onion, celery and bay leaves and simmer for 1 hour. One octopus is sometimes more tender than another, so check to see if yours is cooked after 50 minutes. Use a sharp, pointed knife and poke the octopus – if the knife passes through the flesh easily, it is ready. Remove from the pan, peel off the outer skin and cut the flesh into 2 cm (½ in) cubes.

Meanwhile, bring a pan of salted water to the boil and cook the potatoes. Drain, peel and cut them into slices.

In a large bowl, mix together the potato slices, lemon juice, olive oil, parsley and chilli, and season with salt and pepper.

Add the octopus to the potatoes and mix gently together, so that the dressing coats everything thoroughly. Transfer to serving plates and serve with crusty white bread.

desserts

AND PRESERVES

roasted fruits • fig and orange upside-down cake • plum crostata • hazelnut meringue biscuits • panforte • dark chocolate semifreddo with hot white chocolate sauce • chocolate, cinnamon and pear tart • vin santo and honey ice cream • limoncello granita • peach ripple ice cream • livia's easy peach jam

desserts and preserves

Giancarlo loves cooking savoury dishes, so he let's me make all the puddings at home and in our cookery school. To gather ideas for our Tuscan course, I asked Livia whether she had any recipes for desserts, although I knew she made most of hers from memory. I thought she might have an ancient book hidden away, filled with instructions on how to make fascinating Tuscan puddings and cakes. She reached up and pulled down a dusty old jar, from high up on a shelf and, lo and behold, handed me a stash of old bits of paper with recipes scribbled on them.

The tale of the Tuscan sponge

I was very excited. I went through them one by one, copying them out and imagining the desserts I would make – and the book of undiscovered recipes I would write. Although there were no pictures to go by, often just a list of ingredients and no instructions, I translated and wrote. After a while, it became apparent that the ingredients were similar: eggs, sugar and flour with the addition of orange, chocolate, even coconut. In fact, each recipe was a variation on a basic one – for sponge cake! Yes, Livia had given me 26 recipes for sponge cake. I knew Tuscany wasn't famous for its desserts but this was ridiculous.

I was determined to find out more about the region's desserts, so I visited Gina, Giancarlo's aunt, who taught me her two favourite ones. They sounded lovely when she described them to me, so I was surprised when I arrived in her kitchen to find eggs, sugar, flour – and little else on the table. She asked me to go into the garden and pick the plums her husband, Alfredo, couldn't reach, so at least I knew one

pudding had plums in it. I watched dutifully while Gina whisked, sieved and stirred. The first dish turned out to be made in a ring mould and contained potato flour and a little lemon as well as the basic sponge ingredients on the table. It was turned out on to a plate and was, in fact, a sponge cake. The second also became a sponge – a delicious one, though, and something I hadn't seen since the seventies: an upside-down cake, in this case made with plums. A variation on this, Fig and Orange Upside-down Cake, is on page 124.

In my search for desserts I scoured book shops and questioned patisserie chefs, but the story was always the same. Apart from *panna cotta* (literally, cooked cream), *crostate* and a couple of other exceptions, when it comes to puddings, sponge cakes rule in Tuscany. For the course I included some biscuit and ice-cream recipes, and even looked outside Tuscany for inspiration.

Crostate: Tuscan jam tarts

Crostate – jam-filled tarts with a lattice of pastry strips – are everywhere in Tuscany, particularly in early autumn. To get the best out of the wonderful seasonal fruits we top our *crostate* with the same type of fruit the jam is made from (see Plum Crostata, page 126). This produces a delicious dessert and complements the lightness of the subtly flavoured pastry.

Making jam, Tuscan-style

Tuscans with any land have an *orto* (orchard) and even people with little space in their gardens make room for one or two fruit trees. Plums, or *susine*, typically the *cosce delle suore*

variety, were in season when we were in Tuscany, and peaches were also plentiful, as were figs. Livia (below right with her sister, Albertina) was in full jam-making mode and she invited us to bring our students to her house to help her.

I hadn't realized how popular jam-making is in Tuscany, and had come with jars, lids, pot and pans, bought in London at huge expense. However, the markets and local hardware shops were full of jars and lids in all shapes and sizes. Livia explained, smiling, that everyone in Tuscany makes their own jam. I made it Livia's way to check the timings for the course and was amazed at how easy and straightforward her process is – no pectin, no thermometer, just

centrifugal force in the spinner spins the honey out of the combs. Giorgio then turned the tap at the bottom of the machine and watched as his jar filled to the brim. It was *millefiori* honey, for which the bees collect pollen from various types of flower.

There are many varieties of honey in Tuscany. They include chestnut, which is strong and dark; *melata*, from the gum produced by overripe fruit; *girasole* (sunflower); and the most delicate of all – and the honey of choice for our ice-cream recipe on page 132 – acacia. All are delicious spread thinly on slices of medium-mature pecorino and accompanied by fresh pears or walnuts. For a slightly different use of honey, see the dressing for the White Winter Salad on page 22.

After our honey-making we were invited into the house by Albertina, Livia's sister, who offered us a glass of home-made *vin santo* and a slice of freshly made dessert. Great I thought, this may be the chance to discover another pudding. But you guessed it – it was a nice, dry sponge cake! She offered me the recipe; I politely declined.

fruit, sugar and an oven. Livia's Easy Peach Jam (page 136) is a delicious example of the end result. When we visited her there was plenty of time for the students to make jam, have a walk around her orchard and vegetable garden, and finish the day with a cup of tea. How civilized!

Honey: the taste of sweetness

My son Giorgio loves honey – we have jars of it in various shapes and sizes – so when I was offered the chance to find out more about it, I knew who my companion would be. Francesco, the honey-maker or apiarist, is Livia's brother-in-law. He showed us his beehives and explained how honeycombs are collected. We helped him to scrape off their waxy layers to expose the golden nectar underneath and saw how the

Ice cream: a Roman legacy

The Romans enjoyed ice cream when their empire was at its peak, and Italians still do great ice creams, sorbets, *granite* (water ices) and *semifreddi* (half-frozen ice cream). It is here that they let their imaginations wander and new flavours are constantly being invented. Not many people make ice cream at home, possibly because an ice cream and a cup of coffee, in a caffé on their local piazza, makes an enjoyable ending to a *passagiata*, a stroll.

We have chosen a few of the most popular ice creams we made on the course. Some are best on their own and others, such as Peach Ripple Ice Cream (page 134), are a great accompaniment to other desserts.

This is one of Giancarlo's standby dishes. He makes it whenever we are in need of a quick dessert. It is simple and you can use a variety of seasonal fruits, such as nectarines, damsons, pears and even bananas. We serve it with vanilla ice cream or Vin Santo and Honey Ice Cream (page 132). It is also very good with a dryish dessert, like a nut tart or sponge cake.

roasted fruits

SERVES 4

4 figs, halved

4 plums, halved and stoned

4 peaches, halved, stoned and cut into chunks

2 oranges, quartered

4–5 tablespoons Cointreau or Grand Marnier

Preheat the oven to 200°C/400°F/Gas 6.

Arrange the figs, plums and peaches in a single layer in a roasting tin. Squeeze the juice from the orange quarters over the fruits.

Bake for 20 minutes. Take the tin out of the oven, sprinkle the Cointreau or Grand Marnier over the fruits and bake for a further 5–7 minutes or until all the liqueur has evaporated.

Gina, Giancarlo's aunt, makes this delicious light sponge pudding, torta dello zia, *with whatever fruit is in season. It's very easy to prepare, always works and has become a staple dinner-party favourite of ours. We prefer figs, oranges or plums, but it also works well with apples and poached pears.*

fig and orange upside-down cake

SERVES 8

8 figs, halved, or 4 oranges, peeled
   and sliced
3 large free-range eggs
120 g (4¹⁄₂ oz) caster sugar
1 teaspoon baking powder
2 teaspoons grated orange zest
120 g (4¹⁄₂ oz) plain flour, sifted
Vin Santo and Honey Ice Cream
   (page 132), to serve

FOR THE CARAMEL
200 g (7 oz) granulated sugar

Preheat the oven to 180°C/350°F/Gas 4.

First make the caramel. In a small non-stick pan combine the sugar with 2 teaspoons water over a medium heat until dissolved. Stir and make sure there are no sugar crystals around the edge of the pan. When the sugar mixture is boiling gently and starting to darken, remove the pan from the heat. Pour the caramel into a 20 cm (8 in) flan dish.

Gently push the prepared fruit, cut-sides down, into the caramel in concentric circles. Set aside.

In a mixing bowl, beat the eggs until they have fluffed up to double their size, then gradually beat in the sugar until creamy and thick. Add the baking powder and orange zest and continue to whisk, until the mixture forms thick ribbons. Gradually add the flour. Fold it in carefully to incorporate as much air as possible.

Pour the sponge mixture into the flan dish and bake for 20–30 minutes. Insert a toothpick in the centre of the sponge to see if it is done – if it comes out clean it is ready. Remove from the oven and cut around the sponge with a knife. Wearing your oven gloves, place a serving plate over the top of the tin. Quickly invert the plate and tin, and turn out the sponge – be careful as the caramel will be very hot. Serve warm or at room temperature, with Vin Santo and Honey Ice Cream.

Crostata, *the classic Tuscan dessert, is popular in early autumn when everyone starts to make jam from the summer fruits. My twist is to use fresh plums on top and last year's plum jam underneath. Many fruits work in this way, including fresh peaches with peach jam and fresh figs with fig jam. The pastry is different to the normal shortcrust associated with tarts, as it contains Pane di Angeli, a mixture of baking powder and vanilla powder used frequently by Italians in their desserts. It gives pastry a wonderful light quality and subtle flavour. You'll find it at most Italian delis.*

plum crostata

SERVES 8

350 g (12 oz) plain flour, plus extra
  for dusting
2 eggs
100 g (4 oz) caster sugar
100 g (4 oz) unsalted butter, plus
  extra for greasing
$^1/_2$ teaspoon orange zest
$^1/_2$ teaspoon lemon zest
1 sachet Pane di Angeli or
  1 heaped teaspoon baking
  powder and 4 drops vanilla
  essence, or the seeds from
  $^1/_2$ vanilla pod
300 g (11 oz) plum jam, preferably
  home-made and full-flavoured,
  plus more if needed
egg white or milk, to glaze
8 plums, halved (optional)

Thoroughly mix the flour, eggs, sugar, butter, orange and lemon zest, and Pane di Angeli, baking powder and vanilla essence, or vanilla seeds, to form a firm dough. This can be done in a food processor, or by hand if you prefer– simply squelch the ingredients through your fingers until well blended. Wrap the pastry in cling film and chill in the fridge for 20 minutes.

Preheat the oven to 180°C/350°F/Gas 4. Grease a 25 cm (10 in) loose-bottomed tart tin with butter.

Roll the pastry out on a floured surface to a 30 cm (12 in) circle approximately 5 mm ($^1/_4$ in) thick. Place the pastry in the tart tin, press it gently around the sides and trim. Set aside all the trimmings. Spread with the jam to a depth of at least 2 cm ($^3/_4$ in).

Roll out the trimmings and cut into strips 1 cm ($^1/_2$ in) wide and long enough to cross the tart. Lay these over the tart in a lattice pattern. Brush with a little egg white or milk to glaze. If you're using fresh fruit, omit the pastry lattice and lay the plums neatly on top of the jam.

Bake the tart for 20–25 minutes or until the pastry is light golden in colour. Serve at room temperature. Any leftovers can be kept in an airtight container for a couple of days.

Bruti ma buoni (ugly but good) is the Italian name for these hazelnut meringue biscuits. They are made all over Tuscany and every pasticciere (pastry cook) has his or her own recipe, which they don't entrust to anyone. Giancarlo and I have come up with this version. We trust you with our secret! Just don't tell anyone …

hazelnut meringue biscuits

MAKES ABOUT 30 BISCUITS

250 g (9 oz) hazelnuts
4 egg whites
300 g (11 oz) caster sugar

Preheat the oven to 180°C/350°F/Gas 4. Line a baking tray with greaseproof paper.

Toast the hazelnuts in the oven for a few minutes until they start to brown – watch them carefully to make sure they don't burn. Rub the nuts together in a cloth to remove the skins, then chop finely.

Place the egg whites in a large, clean bowl. Slowly whisk them until they stand in soft peaks. Slowly fold the sugar into the egg whites. Stir in the nuts. Transfer to a pan and cook over a low heat for 30–35 minutes or until the mixture is thick and golden brown. Stir constantly or it will catch on the bottom of the pan.

Remove the pan from the heat and spoon the mixture into mounds about 3 cm (1¼ in) across and 4 cm (1½ in) apart on the baking tray. Bake for 15 minutes, then reduce the temperature to 150°C/300°F/Gas 2 and cook for a further 10 minutes until the colour has deepened.

Remove from the oven and cool on the tray.

When cold, the biscuits can be served straight away or kept in an airtight jar for two to three weeks. They keep very well, so make an excellent present.

Panforte is a Sienese speciality, traditionally made at Christmas. Deliciously gooey, it's packed with nuts and fruits. This version comes from Cesare Beccati, who has a wonderful pastry shop in Siena. It is so popular that Cesare actually makes it all year round now. Italians wrap their panforte in brown paper and tie it with ribbon – stored like this, it will keep for about six months.

panforte

SERVES 10

200 g (7 oz) sugar

100 ml (3½ fl oz) runny honey

375 g (13 oz) assorted candied
   fruit, roughly chopped

200 g (7 oz) almonds, toasted

1 tablespoon plain flour

2 teaspoons ground cinnamon,
   plus extra for dusting

¼ teaspoon freshly grated nutmeg

1 teaspoon freshly ground black
   pepper

¼ teaspoon ground coriander

¼ teaspoon cloves

1 teaspoon ground ginger

1 teaspoon cocoa

icing sugar, for dusting

vin santo or Cointreau, to serve

Preheat the oven to 180°C/350°F/Gas 4. Line a round 25cm/10 in tin with rice paper by placing a circle on the base and strips around the inside rim. It's important that the whole tin is covered.

Combine the sugar and honey with 2 tablespoons water in a large pan and bring to the boil until the temperature reaches 115°C/239°F (use a sugar thermometer to check). Remove from the heat.

Add the candied fruit, almonds, flour, spices and cocoa and stir well. Pour the mixture into the prepared tin. Bake for about 20 minutes, then remove from the oven and cool.

When the panforte is cool, remove from the tin, leaving the rice paper on the panforte. Dust it generously with a mixture of icing sugar and ground cinnamon. Cut into small pieces and serve with *vin santo* or Cointreau.

This recipe is easy to make and the semifreddo *has a rich, bitter chocolate flavour that goes well with the hot white chocolate sauce. It is important to use good-quality chocolate. If you prefer a sweeter ice cream, add a couple of tablespoons of caster sugar to the* semifreddo *before adding the cream. Any leftover sauce will keep in a jar for a couple of weeks. Pour it over summer berries for a totally different dessert.*

dark chocolate semifreddo
with hot white chocolate sauce

SERVES 8

300 g (11 oz) dark chocolate,
  at least 70% cocoa solids
3 tablespoons milk
6 eggs yolks and 3 egg whites
4 tablespoons rum (optional)
300 ml (½ pint) double or
  whipping cream, whipped
sifted cocoa, to dust

FOR THE SAUCE
225 g (8 oz) white chocolate
300 ml (½ pint) double cream

Line a 25 x 14 cm (10 x 5½ in) loaf tin with cling film.

Melt the chocolate and milk in a heatproof bowl placed over a pan of simmering water. Remove from the heat and allow to cool for a couple of minutes.

Gradually beat the egg yolks into the chocolate mixture, then add the rum if using. Fold in the whipped cream. Beat the egg whites until stiff and fold them gently into the cream mixture. Pour into the prepared tin and freeze overnight. Remove the *semifreddo* from the freezer 30 minutes before serving.

To make the sauce, melt the chocolate in a heatproof bowl placed over a pan of simmering water. In another pan, warm the cream until it is hot but not boiling. Remove both pans from the heat. Add the cream to the chocolate and stir well. Pour into a warm jug.

At the last minute, turn out the *semifreddo* and remove the cling film. Sprinkle with a little sifted cocoa and cut into slices. Serve with the sauce.

I was inspired to create this tart after baking a chocolate and pear sponge cake and learning how to make panforte, the spicy Sienese cake. As chocolate and pears go together well, and so do pears and cinnamon, why not combine the three? The tart tastes Christmassy and this is a great recipe for the festive period as it can be made the day before you want to eat it.

chocolate, cinnamon and pear tart

SERVES 6

2 pears, fresh or canned
icing sugar, for dusting
100 g (4 oz) dark chocolate, at
    least 70% cocoa solids, melted
2 eggs, separated
300 g (11 oz) mascarpone
100 g (4 oz) caster sugar
1–2 teaspoons ground cinnamon
large pinch of freshly grated
    nutmeg
large pinch of freshly ground
    black pepper

FOR THE PASTRY
50 g (2 oz) butter, softened, plus
    extra for greasing
100 g (4 oz) plain flour
25 g (1 oz) cocoa
50 g (2 oz) caster sugar
1 egg

TO SERVE
Vin Santo and Honey Ice Cream
    (page 132) or extra mascarpone
fresh redcurrants (optional)

Combine the ingredients for the pastry, in a food processor or by hand in a bowl. When they are well mixed, wrap the pastry in cling film and chill in the fridge for 20 minutes.

Preheat the oven to 180°C/350°F/Gas 4. Grease a 23 cm (9 in) loose-bottomed tart tin with butter.

Peel fresh pears and poach them for 15 minutes in simmering water, then drain. If using canned ones, simply drain.

Remove the pastry from the fridge. Dust the work surface with icing sugar and roll the pastry out to a 28 cm (11 in) circle approximately 5 mm (¼ in) thick. (To stop the pastry sticking to the rolling pin, put cling film between the rolling pin and pastry.) Place the pastry in the tart tin, press it gently around the sides and trim. Prick the bottom all over with a fork.

Bake the pastry case blind (I do this by putting a circle of grease-proof paper over the pastry and covering it with baking beans) for 15 minutes.

While the pastry is cooking, make the filling. Melt the chocolate in a heatproof bowl placed over a pan of gently simmering water. Set aside to cool slightly. Beat the egg yolks and mascarpone until pale and creamy. Add the sugar, cinnamon, nutmeg and pepper and mix well. Pour in the cooled chocolate and stir well.

Whisk the egg whites until they form soft peaks. Fold them lightly into the chocolate mixture using a metal spoon – I find that stirring in a figure-of-eight shape works best – until well incorporated.

Remove the pastry case from the oven and discard the paper and beans.

Cut each pear into eight thick slices. Arrange the slices in a circle on the pastry. Top with the filling and bake for 25–30 minutes, or until a toothpick inserted into the centre of the filling comes away clean. The top should feel firm to the touch and have cracked a little. Leave to cool.

Serve at room temperature with Vin Santo and Honey Ice Cream or mascarpone, and a few redcurrants if you like. If you're making the tart the day before you intend to eat it, store it overnight in the fridge, and remove 30 minutes before serving to take the edge off the coldness.

After our visit to the honey festival in Tuscany (see page 22) Giancarlo and I were inspired to use honey in everything. Combining Nello's home-made vin santo *and his brother-in-law's honey created a heavenly flavour for ice cream that went down a treat in Tuscany. Buy the best quality honey you can find, as the flavour does come through, and if you can't get* vin santo, *use any dessert wine. This ice cream is fabulous with desserts such as Roasted Fruits (page 123) and Fig and Orange Upside-down Cake (page 124).*

vin santo and honey ice cream

SERVES 6

2 eggs
100 g (4 oz) acacia honey
100 ml (3^1/$_2$ fl oz) *vin santo*
300 ml (^{1}/$_2$ pint) double cream

Line a 25 x 14 cm (10 x 5^1/$_2$ in) loaf tin with cling film.

Beat the eggs and honey together in a heatproof bowl placed over a pan of simmering water. Gradually stir in the *vin santo*. Set aside to cool. This is the basic recipe for zabaglione.

Meanwhile, whip the cream until it forms soft peaks. When the zabaglione is cool, fold in the cream.

Pour the mixture into the prepared tin and freeze. Alternatively, transfer it to an ice-cream maker and follow the manufacturer's instructions.

Limoncello is a classic Italian liqueur made with lemons, and the students on our course enjoyed our 'limoncello nights'. As we made our own liqueur from pure alcohol marginally diluted with water, the evenings ended up being quite riotous! This granita is a refreshing way of using limoncello – *it is sharp yet sweet, and is great served between courses to cleanse the palette. Like crunchy snow, it melts quickly, so when ready it should be consumed straight away. It is nice served in shot glasses, topped with a few very thin strips of lemon zest. It is also delicious served as an accompaniment to a selection of fresh summer berries.*

limoncello granita

**MAKES 12 SMALL OR
6 LARGE SERVINGS**

1 lemon
100 g (4 oz) caster sugar
350 ml (12 fl oz) *limoncello*

Finely peel the lemon to remove the zest, and set this aside for decoration. Squeeze the juice from the lemon and place in a pan.

Add 1 litre (1³/₄ pints) water and the sugar to the lemon juice and boil until the sugar has dissolved.

Remove from the heat, add the *limoncello* and set aside to cool. When cool, pour into a flat container and freeze until crystals form around the edge.

At this point, stir the mixture vigorously with a fork, then put it back in the freezer.

Repeat this process every 30 minutes over the next few hours until there is no liquid in the container – just crunchy, broken crystals of ice. Leave the granita in the freezer until needed. Serve in individual glasses, decorated with lemon zest.

This is a refreshing fruity summer ice cream. Although it's made with ripe, fresh peaches, Giancarlo and I like even more intense flavours, so we use some of Livia's Easy Peach Jam (page 136). The result is delicious, especially when served with a slice of peach-jam filled Crostata (page 126).

peach ripple ice cream

SERVES 8

4 ripe peaches, peeled, stoned
    and cut into chunks
250 g (9 oz) mascarpone
200 ml (7 fl oz) milk
200 g (7 oz) caster sugar
3 tablespoons *limoncello*, vodka
    or peach schnapps
1 jar Livia's Easy Peach Jam
    (page 136) or 1 × 300 ml jar
    of bought soft-set jam,
    plus extra to serve

Combine all the ingredients, except the jam, in a food processor. Pour into a large container and freeze for a couple of hours until crystals start to form.

Remove and stir well to break up the crystals. Return to the freezer. Repeat twice more – the last time, stir in the jam.

Alternatively, pour into an ice-cream maker and churn, following the manufacturer's instructions. Stir in the jam at the end.

This is quite a soft ice cream, so you can serve it straight from the freezer, with a little extra jam spooned over.

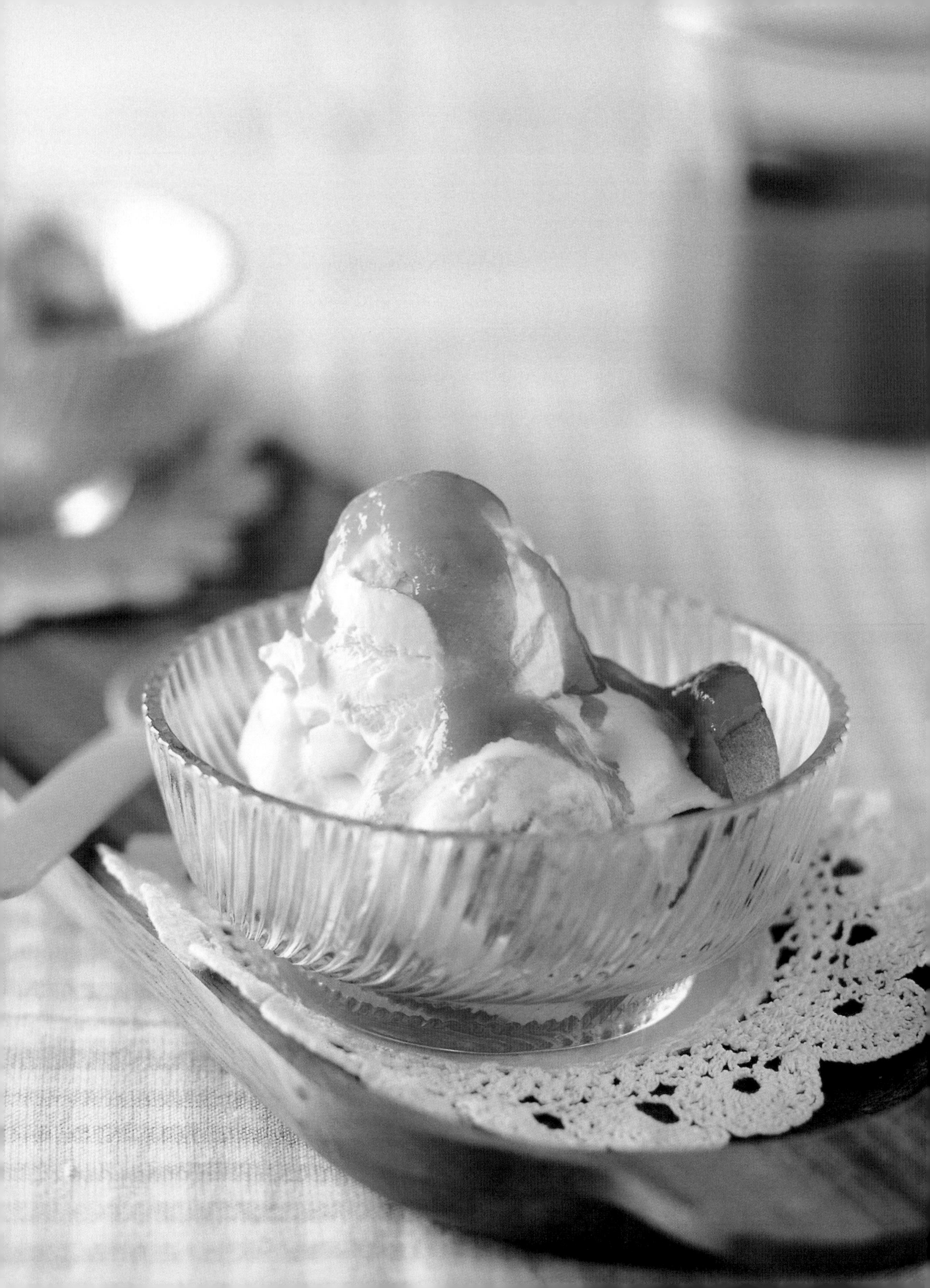

Livia and her husband, Nello, make jam in a wood-burning stove (right) that they move from their garage to their garden, depending on the weather. This adds a wonderful woody flavour to their jam – we make ours in a domestic oven and it is just as good. It is quite a runny, soft-set jam, which means it's perfect for cooking, but not so great for toast or muffins. If the jam is made with fruit in season, the flavour is usually sweet enough not to need sugar, but Livia adds some to help preserve the fruit. The jam will keep for up to a year and is great for using in Crostata (page 126) and Peach Ripple Ice Cream (page 134), and for giving away as presents – so make as much as you can cook or store.

livia's easy peach jam

**MAKES ENOUGH TO FILL FOUR
300 ML (½ PINT) JARS**

1.5 kg (3¼ lb) peaches, peeled,
  halved and stoned
juice of 2 lemons
200–250 g (7–9 oz) granulated or
  caster sugar

Preheat the oven to 200°C/400°F/Gas 6.

Cut away any coarse red spiky flesh in the areas where the stones were removed. The red would spoil the colour of the finished jam. Cut off any discoloured flesh. Put the peaches in a large preserving pan or ovenproof dish. Pour over the lemon juice and mix well. Bake for 40–60 minutes or until the peaches have softened, stirring every 10 minutes. Leave to cool slightly.

Purée the cooled peaches, either in a food processor or by passing them through a *passatutto* (food mill), then return them to the preserving pan or ovenproof dish. Stir in enough sugar to sweeten them to your taste. Return the jam to the oven for another 30 minutes, stirring every 10 minutes.

Meanwhile, sterilize four jars and lids by washing them in very hot soapy water or in a dishwasher. Place them in the oven for a couple of minutes to warm up. This will prevent them cracking when the hot jam is poured into them.

Remove the jam from the oven and immediately pour it through a funnel into the jars. Leave a 2 cm ($^3/_4$ in) gap at the top of each jar and screw the lids on tightly. The gap is crucial as it will form a vacuum when the jars are reheated.

Put a *bain-marie* or roasting tin large enough to hold all the jars on the hob. Stand the jars in it and pour in enough water to cover them completely. Boil for 20–30 minutes, then remove the jars and leave them to cool. Store in a dark cupboard, away from direct heat.

variation

To make plum jam, preheat the oven to 160°C/325°F/Gas 3. Put 2 kg (4$^1/_2$ lb) plums, halved and stoned, into a preserving pan or ovenproof dish large enough to take all of them in one layer. Bake as for Livia's Easy Peach Jam until the plums have softened.

Purée the plums, add 25–50 g (1–2 oz) caster sugar, and return the jam to the oven for another 20 minutes. Stir the jam once after 10 minutes. Now follow the instructions for Livia's Easy Peach Jam.

This will make enough jam to fill about five 300 ml ($^1/_2$ pint) jars.

bread

AND PIZZA

quick focaccia • traditional focaccia • pane toscano • breadsticks • torta al testo • thin oven-baked pizza • focaccia stuffed with mozarella • pan' co' santi

bread and pizza

I never thought I would say so, but I am mad about baking bread! I first learnt to make it when I was at school, but it never really worked and I was put off trying for years until a passionate bread enthusiast, Ursula Ferrigno, started teaching at our cookery school. She made it seem so easy that I instantly fell in love with making my own bread and have never looked back. So, if you have never tried, please give it a go!

Our house seems even more of a home when it smells of freshly baked bread, and both children love to bake, especially Giorgio, who is a bread fiend like me. We eat it toasted, spread with garlic oil, soaked in a soup and made into sandwiches. We make a variety of breads including wholemeal and white loaves, focaccia, pizza, *grissini* (breadsticks) and *testo* bread. As a child, Giancarlo often made *ciaccia* with his mother – *ciaccia* is the Tuscan nickname for focaccia.

Italy is home to a huge range of breads that vary from region to region and differ again within each region. I found the wonderful nut-filled *pan' co' santi* in Siena – Giancarlo had never heard of it – but it was unavailable just 40 miles away in Montepulciano. The names also differ, even though the recipes hardly change – in Florence focaccia is known as *schiachiata*.

Italians eat bread with everything, at the beginning of a meal and with the main course. They mop up the juices on their plates with what they call a *scarpetta* (slipper) because of its shape. Bread is also used in a stuffing for chicken and to thicken soups such as Ribollita (page 51). In *spaghetti alla bricole*, instead of a

sauce breadcrumbs are mixed with garlic and chillies and tossed with the cooked spaghetti.

Pane Toscano: bread without salt

My least favourite Italian bread is *pane Toscano*, the big white loaf made without salt. When you tear off a piece and eat it, the texture is fine and the crust delicious, but bread without salt somehow always tastes disappointing. Tuscan bakers decided not to use it in their bread in the sixteenth century because of ludicrously high taxes on salt imposed by the Papal States.

We saw just how precious salt became when we visited Sylvia who lives in the local *casa collonica*, the Italian version of a manor house. There's a separate little wooden salt door at the side of her house. It was here that salt was taken in from the 'brigands', brave men who brought their precious commodity along the road from the sea, protecting their cargo from bandits. She explained that no one wanted the brigands to enter their houses, so the salt was passed through a tiny doorway and money was passed back to them. Sylvia told us that salt was so precious that farmers would not have wasted it on bread; they needed it more urgently to preserve meat. Since those times have long

passed, you would think Tuscans would have added salt to their bread again. However, change comes slowly in Tuscany … Tuscans believe the saltiness of their *salumi* and food generally more than makes up for the absence of salt in bread. Our *pane Toscano* (page 148) includes salt as an optional extra, and it works well. It seems a shame not to enjoy this otherwise wonderful loaf.

Pane Toscano was traditionally made every 10–14 days in an *armadia*, a wooden chest with a flat area on which the dough was prepared. A lid dropped down to keep the space inside draught-free while the loaves were proved. After baking, the bread was kept in this same area. Ingredients were stored in a cupboard underneath. The lack of salt in the bread made a hard loaf that dried quickly when it was broken up, but whole loaves could be kept for up to two weeks.

Testo: a flat bread

Testo – 'bread of the tile' – really an Umbrian speciality, is a flat bread cooked over a *testo* (stone or iron) and served hot, stuffed with cheese, meat or vegetables (see page 150 for our recipe and suggestions for fillings). Giancarlo's home town of Montepulciano

Stazione is near the border between Tuscany and Umbria around Lake Trasimeno. We love going to the caffé there to watch the bread being cooked over hot stones. The stones are heated in a roaring fire and are then brought out and used to cook the bread. When they cool down they are returned to the fire.

Focaccia: bread from the hearth

Focaccia (above), originally from Liguria, used to be made in the hearth near the fire or *fuoco*, hence its name. It should be light and slightly spongy with a salty oiliness on top. It can be plain and sprinkled just with salt, or have salt and herbs, or almost any other ingredient, scattered over it. Focaccia can be stuffed with cheese and herbs before or after cooking. There is even a sweet version made with grapes and sugar. No matter where you are in Italy, the proportion of flour to liquid remains more or less the same, but the liquid can be milk, half milk and half water, or just water. Various flours are used in each region, from chick-pea flour to half semolina flour and half white bread flour. Tuscans make focaccia with white bread flour and water. The dough is very versatile and once mastered it can be used to make pizza, *grissini* and garlic bread.

The ingredients

Flour, water, yeast, salt and sometimes oil are the staple ingredients in bread. Although they are not hard to find, they differ in most countries. For a start, the water is different in Tuscany and is not like the water where we live in central London. For this reason it is essential to be adaptable when making bread. I prefer to use strong white bread flour but this is different according to the brand and its country of origin. Add more or less flour or water to adjust the consistency. And don't be surprised if one type of flour absorbs a great deal more water than another.

I am often asked what 0 and 00 flour are. The '0' rating is used to describe how finely the flour is milled. Many people, including Italians, mistakenly think that 0 is strong flour and 00 is soft flour, but it's not as simple as that. The Italians don't measure their flour in terms of protein, which, when combined with water creates gluten, which is necessary to make bread. Flours milled from soft wheat just don't have the elasticity required for bread-making, whereas 0 and 00 flours could contain high or low levels of gluten depending on the brand.

It comes down to personal preference which flour to use. Giancarlo prefers 00 flour for making pasta, as it's lighter and finer. Livia prefers 0 flour for both focaccia and pasta. Both flours will work, but give a slightly different result. They both agree, however, that 00 flour is generally better for cakes and *biscotti*.

When buying flour in the UK, look out for those milled specifically for bread- or pasta-making, which are sold in most supermarkets.

Fresh versus dried yeast

Yeast is a single-celled fungus that converts sugar and starch into alcohol and bubbles of carbon dioxide. In baking the tiny bubbles become trapped in the dough and make the bread rise so that it is light and airy when cooked. The alcohol is burnt off during the baking process.

I prefer fresh yeast (*lievito di birra*) to dried. Anything that is natural and has not been processed seems better to me. However, performance-wise, dried yeast works just as well and I always have some in my cupboard as a back-up. As a general rule you need twice as much fresh as dried yeast. Dried yeast comes in two forms; active and instant. Instant needs only one rising, which certainly saves time, and should be added straight to the flour without first being mixed with water.

Fresh yeast is available from some delis, small bakeries and the bakery departments in large supermarkets, but you have to ask for it. In Italy it can be bought in small pieces, but in the UK it is often easier to buy a large piece and cut it into individual portions. These can be frozen for up to six months. Defrost an hour before use or if, like me, you forget to do this, break up the unforgiving frozen lump and the warm water used to make the bread will soon bring it back to life again. Once defrosted, the yeast can be kept in the fridge for about three days.

How to use a *biga* (starter)

When we returned to Tuscany to run the cookery school I had been making bread in London for a year or so, using recipes from our patisserie chefs at the Caffé Caldesi. I was looking forward to working with cooks and bakers in Tuscany and seeing how they made bread. I began my quest to make the perfect focaccia!

I understood that to get a really tasty focaccia you start with a starter or *biga*. This gives any bread a richer flavour and, some say, a better crust. Ursula talks about the eyes – holes – in her ciabatta that are created by the *biga* made a couple of days earlier.

Before yeast could be bought as a separate entity, a *biga* was made by making a paste with flour and water and leaving it for a day or so at room temperature. During this time natural airborne yeasts got into the paste and started to reproduce. The *biga* was kept alive in a container stored in a cool place. A piece – never all of it – was taken out and used, and was replaced by more flour and water. In this way a *biga* could be kept for years. Another method was to use the natural yeast derived from grape must.

Nowadays, a starter can be made by adding bought yeast to the paste of flour and water. Some recipes suggest making this type of starter just half an hour before using it; others recommend making it up to three days in advance.

We tested focaccia with and without a *biga*, and the one with it (Traditional Focaccia, page 146) was voted the best – but only just. Our simple Quick Focaccia (page 144) made from scratch and not using a starter, was also delicious.

Find the right place for rising

The secret of good bread is in the rising – the process must not be rushed – and it is essential to find a place in your home where the dough can be left for the necessary length of time. In Tuscany we put it above the coffee machine where it is always warm. In the UK it goes in the airing cupboard above the tumble-dryer, and my mother leaves her dough above the boiler. The place must be draught-free and if it is slightly warm the rising process will be quicker.

Hand or machine?

In the UK I generally use a food processor to save time but I'm happy to use my hands if necessary. Unlike a machine, they create warmth and this results in a better dough. According to Vito Volpi, a retired baker who

taught us in Tuscany, the warmth starts the rising process even before you have finished kneading.

Kneading

Every professional and amateur baker seems to have a slightly different way of kneading. They all work provided you actually stretch the dough. Poking, pushing and prodding won't work. Kneading should be the equivalent of exercising your arms and hands.

What kind of oven?

In Tuscany, we used the hotel's fan oven for baking – it was only a little bigger than an average domestic one. The focaccia and the other breads worked every time and we developed a way of making pizza in it, instead of using a wood-burning or bread oven. Our students were pleased that they would be able to make delicious home-made bread and pizza when they returned home without needing any special equipment.

Originally from Liguria, this delicious bread is now made all over Italy in various forms. Focaccia is simple to make, by hand or in an electric mixer with a dough hook.

quick focaccia

SERVES 8–10

2 heaped teaspoons fresh yeast
   or 1½ teaspoons dried yeast
300 ml (½ pint) tepid water
500 g (1 lb 2 oz) 0 flour or strong
   white bread flour, plus extra for
   dusting
1½ teaspoons salt
5–6 tablespoons extra-virgin
   olive oil, plus extra for greasing
medium-coarse sea salt
leaves torn from 2 sprigs fresh
   rosemary

Combine the yeast with 2 tablespoons tepid water, stir well and leave for 5 minutes to soften and dissolve.

Put the flour and salt in a large mixing bowl and make a well in the centre. Add the yeast and water mixture and 3 tablespoons olive oil and mix thoroughly. Gradually add the remaining water to make a sticky dough.

Turn the dough out on to a floured surface, gathering all the pieces of dough from the edge of the bowl and leaving it clean. Knead for about 10 minutes, adding a little extra flour if necessary, until the dough is smooth and elastic and no longer sticks to your hands. To see if it's ready, pull off a piece of dough and stretch it – it should be elastic enough not to break quickly.

Grease a bowl with oil. Transfer the dough to the bowl and cover it with a damp tea towel or oiled cling film. Leave in a warm place until double in size – this will take about 1½ hours depending on the temperature.

Knock the dough back by punching it and knead for a further 2 minutes. Leave to rest for 10 minutes. Oil a baking tray that measures 40 × 30 cm (16 × 12 in) and is 2.5 cm (1 in) deep.

Place the dough on the tray and press it out to the edges. Cover with a tea towel and leave in a warm place until double in size – this will take about 30 minutes, depending on the temperature. Meanwhile, preheat the oven to 200°C/400°F/Gas 6.

Push your fingertips gently into the dough to make indentations and drizzle with the remaining oil. Sprinkle with sea salt and push the rosemary leaves hard into the dough. Bake for 25–35 minutes or until the top is crusty and the bread is cooked through to the base – if you tap it on the bottom, it will sound hollow.

A biga (starter) improves the texture of the bread, making it lighter and more airy. You need to plan ahead for this recipe, as the biga should be started one or two days before the rest of the bread. The longer it is left, the better the crust and flavour of the bread.

traditional focaccia

SERVES 8–10

2 heaped teaspoons fresh yeast
  or 1¹/₂ teaspoons dried yeast
150 ml (¹/₂ pint) tepid water
375 g (13 oz) 0 flour or strong
  white bread flour, plus extra
  for dusting
1¹/₂ teaspoons salt
5–6 tablespoons extra-virgin
  olive oil, plus extra for greasing
medium-coarse sea salt
leaves torn from 2 sprigs fresh
  rosemary

FOR THE STARTER
1 heaped teaspoon fresh yeast
120 ml (4¹/₂ fl oz) tepid water
120 g (4¹/₂ oz) strong white bread
  flour

FOR THE FILLING (OPTIONAL)
grilled peppers
mozzarella slices
basil leaves

To make the starter, combine the yeast with a little tepid water. Put the flour in a bowl and stir in the yeast and water mixture. Gradually add the remaining water and mix with the flour to form a thick paste. Cover with a tea towel and leave at room temperature for 1–2 days. The paste will start to bubble after a short while and smell of beer. If you are working in a hot, dry place – like Tuscany – moisten the tea towel before covering the starter. This will help to prevent a crust forming. Discard any crust that does form and use the fresh starter underneath.

To make the dough, combine the yeast with 2 tablespoons tepid water. Leave for 5 minutes to soften and dissolve.

Put the flour and salt in a large mixing bowl and make a well in the centre. Add the yeast and water mixture, the starter and 3 tablespoons olive oil and mix thoroughly. Gradually add the remaining water to make a sticky dough.

Continue as for Quick Focaccia (page 144) but bake for 25–30 minutes. Eat the bread as it is, or cut in half and fill with grilled peppers, mozzarella and basil – perfect for a picnic!

alternative toppings

Focaccia can be topped with a wide variety of ingredients just before cooking. Both this one and Quick Focaccia (page 144) use rosemary, but you can try combinations of any of the following: fresh thyme, sliced cheese, sliced sausage, halved olives, sun-dried tomatoes, sage leaves, red onion – the possibilities are endless!

This recipe for the saltless Tuscan loaf comes from Vito Volpi who had been a baker all his life. The texture is great, the crust delicious. If you prefer, you can add a couple of teaspoons of salt. The starter should be made a day in advance so a little fore-thought is necessary; otherwise it is an easy bread to make. Tuscans eat it throughout the day, with every meal. Be prepared to be flexible as to how long it will take the dough to rise – it rises in half an hour in a hot country, but take over two hours in a cold one.

pane toscano

MAKES ONE LARGE LOAF

2 tablespoons fresh yeast or
   1 tablespoon dried
300 ml (½ pint) tepid water
1 kg (2¼ lb) strong, white flour,
   plus extra for sprinkling
2 teaspoons salt (optional)

FOR THE STARTER

1 dessertspoon fresh yeast or
   7 g sachet dried yeast
200 ml (7 fl oz) tepid water
250 g (9 oz) strong white bread
   flour

To make the starter, combine the yeast with the tepid water. Put the flour in a bowl and stir in the yeast mixture to make a thick paste. Cover with a tea towel and leave overnight at room temperature.

To make the dough, combine the yeast with 2 tablespoons tepid water. Pour the flour, and salt if using, into a mound on the table. Mix well. Make a well in the centre and add the starter and yeast mixture. Gradually add the remaining water and combine all the ingredients using your hands. Knead the dough for about 10 minutes until it is soft but firm and elastic. Make sure the dough is not too soft – if it is, it will not hold its shape. Add more flour or water if necessary. The dough is ready if it springs back when you push your finger into it.

Divide the dough into two and shape into two round loaves. Place on a 40 × 30 cm (16 × 12 in) baking tray or in a roasting tin. Cut a cross in the top of each loaf and sprinkle lightly with flour. Leave to rise in a warm place until double in size – this will take about 1½ hours, depending on the temperature of the room. Towards the end of the proving time, heat the oven to 200°C/400°F/Gas 6.

Bake for 1 hour or until the loaves sound hollow when tapped underneath. Leave to cool on a wire rack.

Salvatore Giannetti, who was a pasticciere (pastry cook) in Naples, provided this recipe for grissini, Italy's classic breadsticks. Everyone in our family finds them irresistible, with their moreish Parmesan flavour. Like many Tuscans, Giancarlo often wraps them in very thin slices of prosciutto. For a party it's good to make some with herbs and some without. Leftover breadsticks can be stored in an airtight container for a few days.

breadsticks

MAKES ABOUT 40 BREADSTICKS

25 g (1 oz) fresh yeast or
  20 g ($^3/_4$ oz) dried yeast
300 ml ($^1/_2$ pint) tepid milk
750 g (1 lb 10 oz) strong white
  bread flour, plus extra for dusting
20 g ($^3/_4$ oz) salt
50 g (2 oz) Parmesan, freshly grated
100 g (4 oz) butter, softened
oil, for greasing
chopped fresh rosemary leaves or
  thyme leaves (optional)

Combine the yeast with 2 tablespoons tepid milk, stir well and leave for 5 minutes to dissolve.

Put the flour, salt and Parmesan into a bowl and mix well.

Rub the butter into the dry ingredients until the mixture resembles breadcrumbs. Stir in the yeast and milk mixture. Gradually add the remaining milk to form a soft dough. Turn out onto a floured surface and knead for about 10 minutes. The dough should be soft and elastic. Grease a bowl with oil. Transfer the dough to the bowl, smear it with a little more oil and cover it with cling film. Leave in a warm place until double in size – this will take about $1^1/_2$ hours depending on the temperature.

When the dough is ready, knock it back by punching it, then on a clean surface (don't use flour) roll it out into sausage shapes about 2 cm ($^3/_4$ in) across and the length of a baking tray. You can plait three strips together or make heart shapes – the possibilities are endless. Roll the strips or shapes in the chopped herbs, if using. Divide them between two baking trays and leave in a warm place for another 20 minutes or so until they have swollen and become slightly puffy. Meanwhile, preheat the oven to 240°C/475°F/Gas 9.

Bake for about 10–15 minutes, until the breadsticks are deep golden. They are ready when they snap easily and are no longer squashy inside. Leave to cool on a wire rack.

Testo breads are traditionally cooked over a stone or piece of cast iron heated over glowing embers or a gas stove. They cook in minutes and are served split open and stuffed. Giancarlo cooks them in a hot, dry frying pan, but that method is a little tricky and he often burns the pan! I have developed a way of cooking them in a domestic oven that produces a wonderful result. The baking powder makes the bread puff up quickly.

torta al testo

MAKES 12 BREADS

750 g (1 lb 10 oz) strong white
  bread flour, plus extra for dusting
4 tablespoons oil
2 teaspoons salt
40 g (1¹/₂ oz) baking powder

FOR THE FILLING
your choice of rocket, radicchio,
  fresh spinach leaves, mozzarella,
  pecorino, cooked sausage,
  prosciutto
drizzle of olive oil
salt and freshly ground black
  pepper

Put two baking sheets in the oven and set the oven at its highest setting. The baking sheets must be so hot that the breads cook as soon as they touch them.

Mix the flour, oil, salt and baking powder together. Gradually add 500 ml (18 fl oz) water to form a soft dough – you may not need all the water. This can be done in a food processor with a dough hook or by hand in a bowl.

Turn the dough out on to a floured suface and knead for 10 minutes, folding the dough inwards on itself until soft and elastic. Divide the dough into 12 even-sized pieces. Roll each one out into a circle about the size of your hand and leave to rest for 5 minutes to relax the dough.

Roll out again into 15 cm (6 in) circles, 5 mm (¹/₄ in) thick. Immediately put four on each hot baking sheet. Return to the oven and bake for 5–7 minutes until golden and puffed up, turning the breads over halfway.

Remove from the oven and leave to cool for a couple of minutes. Split the breads open using a knife to prize the sides apart and fill with your choice of ingredients. Eat straight away or, if you have chosen cheese, return to the oven for a couple of minutes to melt it.

Cook the remaining four breads in the same way and serve.

Quick, easy, crispy-based pizza that can be cooked in a domestic oven and never fails to impress – what more could you want? This recipe was a staple of our Tuscan cookery course.

thin oven-baked pizza

SERVES 4–6

olive oil, for greasing
$^1/_2$ quantity Quick Focaccia dough (page 144), prepared to the stage where it has risen in the bowl
300 ml ($^3/_4$ pint) passata
200 g (7 oz) mozzarella, cut into 2 cm ($^3/_4$ in) cubes
1 teaspoon dried oregano
12 black olives
1 garlic clove, chopped (optional)
salt and freshly ground black pepper
handful of basil leaves, torn, to serve

Preheat the oven to 240°C/475°C/Gas 9 and grease a 40 × 30 cm (16 × 12 in) baking sheet with a little olive oil.

Knock the dough back by punching it, and leave it to rest for 5 minutes.

On a floured surface, roll the dough out as thinly as you can – it should be about 2 mm ($^1/_8$ in) thick – to fit the baking sheet.

Gently lay the dough on the baking sheet and press it out to the edges. The dough is delicate at this stage but will be very strong when it's cooked.

Spread the passata thinly over the dough. Scatter with the mozzarella, oregano and olives, and garlic if using. Season.

Place on the highest shelf of the oven and bake for 10–15 minutes. Don't be tempted to take the pizza out too soon – as long as the cheese is not burning, the pizza will improve by becoming crispy.

The pizza is ready when it looks crispy and the mozzarella has melted. Cut it into squares and serve topped with basil leaves.

very crispy garlic and rosemary pizza bread

On one of our courses we had some leftover pizza dough. As we were in frugal Tuscany, instead of discarding it we rolled it out thinly, placed it on a baking sheet, covered it with olive oil and a little sea salt and cooked it for 10 minutes. Then we scattered chopped garlic and rosemary on top and put it back in the oven. Unfortunately I forgot it was there! The crispy burnt offerings were surprisingly delicious, however, and a hit with our students. Although I cooked mine for longer, I recommend cooking this for no more than 15 minutes until golden brown and crisp. Don't forget to set your timer!

We have tried various stuffings for focaccia, and oozing melted cheese is always a popular choice. You could try something stronger like Gorgonzola or fontina if you prefer.

focaccia stuffed with mozzarella

SERVES 8–10

1 quantity Quick Focaccia dough (page 144), prepared to the stage where it has risen in the bowl

2–3 tablespoons extra-virgin olive oil, plus extra for greasing

flour, for dusting

175 g (6 oz) mozzarella, chopped into 2 cm ($^3/_4$ in) cubes

8 basil leaves, roughly torn

6 sun-dried tomatoes, roughly chopped

medium-coarse sea salt and freshly ground black pepper

leaves torn from 2 sprigs fresh rosemary

Knock the dough back by punching it and leave it to rest for 10 minutes.

Oil a baking tray. Halve the dough, place one half on the baking tray and shape it into an oval about 1 cm ($^1/_2$ in) deep. Put the mozzarella, basil leaves and sun-dried tomatoes on top. Season with salt and pepper.

Roll out the remaining dough on a floured surface to make an oval the same size as the first one. Place it on top of the first oval and press down round the edges to seal it. Cover with a tea towel and leave in a warm place until double in size – this will take about 30 minutes. Meanwhile, preheat the oven to 200°C/400°F/Gas 6.

Push your fingertips gently into the dough to make indentations and drizzle with the olive oil. Sprinkle with sea salt and push the rosemary leaves hard into the dough. Bake for 25–35 minutes or until the top is crusty and the bread is cooked through to the base. To check, lift one corner of the stuffed focaccia while it's still in the tin – it should be crisp underneath, not soggy.

This is a wonderfully nutty, fruity loaf, traditionally made for the Day of the Dead on 2 November, and eaten plain, with coffee. Cesare Buccati, who has a pastry shop in Siena, doesn't use spices, just a pinch of black pepper, but Vito Volpi, our baker friend, uses cinnamon. Giancarlo and I like spices, so this version also has nutmeg. Try experimenting with your favourite spices.

pan' co' santi

MAKES 2 LOAVES

100 g (4 oz) lard, butter or margarine, plus extra for greasing
375 g (13 oz) strong white bread flour, plus extra for dusting
50 g (2 oz) caster sugar
2 teaspoons salt
good pinch of freshly ground black pepper
1 teaspoon ground cinnamon
$^1/_2$ teaspoon freshly grated nutmeg
175 ml (6 fl oz) tepid water
300 g (11 oz) walnuts, shelled and skinned
500 g (1 lb 2 oz) raisins

FOR THE STARTER
15 g ($^1/_2$ oz) fresh yeast or 7 g sachet dried yeast
125 ml ($4^1/_2$ fl oz) tepid water
125 g ($4^1/_2$ oz) strong white bread flour

FOR THE GLAZE
1 teaspoon sugar

Grease a large baking tray with the lard, butter or margarine.

Combine all the ingredients for the starter in a large mixing bowl, stir well and leave for 20 minutes. The mixture will start to bubble and expand.

Stir all the ingredients for the dough, except the tepid water, nuts and raisins, into the starter and mix thoroughly. Gradually add the water and stir well to form an sticky dough.

Knead the dough on a floured surface for 10 minutes. Gradually add the nuts and raisins.

Divide the dough into two and shape into two round loaves. Place the loaves on the baking tray and cut a cross in the top of each. Cover with a tea towel and leave in a warm, draught-free place until double in size – this will take $1^1/_2$–2 hours depending on the temperature. Towards the end of the proving time, heat the oven to 180°C/350°F/Gas 4.

To make the glaze, heat 1 tablespoon water, add the sugar and stir until dissolved. Once the dough has risen, brush the loaves with the sugar and water mixture.

Bake for 40–50 minutes or until the loaves sound hollow when tapped underneath. Leave to cool on a wire rack. Some of the raisins from the outside will have perished in the baking – brush these off before serving.

menu suggestions

Al fresco buffet lunch for a crowd
- Breadsticks (page 149)
- Tomato Bruschetta (page 24)
- Focaccia filled with mozzarella, roasted red pepper and basil (pages 144–7)
- Salted Sardines with Chopped Red Onion (page 21)
- Bresaola, Rocket and Parmesan Rolls (page 25)
- Gregorio's Aubergine Slices (page 28)
- Stuffed Chillies (page 29)
- Warm Octopus, Potato and Lemon Salad (page 116 – *see opposite top right for picture*)
- Simple green salad dressed with balsamic vinegar and extra-virgin olive oil
- Peach Ripple Ice Cream (page 134 – *see opposite below right for picture*)

Summer lunch party for four
- Oven-roasted Vegetables with Crumbled Goats' Cheese, Thyme and Parsley (page 31)
- Oven-baked Sea Bream with Tuscan Herb Stuffing (page 112)
- Roasted Fruits (page 123) and vanilla ice cream

Winter dinner party
- White Winter Salad with Honey Dressing (page 22)
- Wild Boar with Chocolate (page 100)
- Luciano's Roast Potatoes (page 37)
- Sformato of Carrots (page 34)
- Green Beans in Tomato Sauce (page 37)
- Plum Crostata (page 126)
- Vin Santo and Honey Ice Cream (page 132)

Quick after-work entertaining
- Steak Tagliata with Rocket, Parmesan and Balsamic Dressing (page 90 – *see opposite below left for picture*)
- Limoncello Granita (page 133)
- Hazelnut Meringue Biscuits (page 127)

Vegetarian dinner party
- Orchard-keepers' Soup (page 55)
- White Lasagne (page 75)
- Focaccia (pages 144–7)
- Fig and Orange Upside-down Cake (page 124)
- Vin Santo and Honey Ice Cream (page 132)

Tuscan-style Christmas celebration
- Balsamic Onions (page 26 – *see opposite top left for picture*) and mixed antipasti platter (pages 16–20)
- Black Crostini (page 32)
- Gregorio's Chestnut and Lentil Soup (page 52)
- Roast Pheasant and Guinea Fowl in Terracotta (page 99)
- Chocolate, Cinnamon and Pear Tart (page 130)
- Pan' co' santi (page 155) and cheeses
- Panforte (page 128) and coffee

Cooking with children
- Mixed antipasti platter (pages 16–20)
- Thin Oven-baked Pizza (page 152)
- Dark Chocolate Semifreddo with Hot White Chocolate Sauce (page 129)

To our mothers, for their love of cooking

ACKNOWLEDGEMENTS

A big thank you to all those intrepid students who came to Tuscany in 2005 for our first cooking course in Italy. We enjoyed a journey of discovery together, searching out and trying local recipes, sharing knowledge, efforts, food and laughter and, above all, learning. Without them there would have been no course, no television series and no book. So thank you to one and all.

We would like to thank Siobhan Browne for being such an invaluable friend and for her support while we wrote this book, from following up late-night research queries to looking after our children while we were glued to the computer.

Thank you to Adam Alexander, Sheila Ableman, Nicky Ross and Stuart Cooper for believing in the book; to Sarah Reece and Isobel Gillan for their patience, skill and perfectionism; to Jan Baldwin for her wonderful food photographs – her passion and dedication were an inspiration; and to Jesse Alexander for his lovely location shots.

We have been so touched by the extra efforts our staff at the restaurants have made to help us perfect and practise recipes, especially Gregorio Piazza, Stefano Borella, Jo Hynes and Marta Federico.

Our gratitude, too, to all those unwitting recipe-testers who came round for dinner and found themselves helping us cook and test new dishes, including Emma Oxley, Susie Marquis, Jo Randall, Katie's parents and Katie's brother, Philip Beresford.

Finally we would like to apologize to Giorgio and Flavio for letting them watch too much television and eat too much chocolate while this book was written. Sometimes bribery is necessary when deadlines have to be met!

This book is published to accompany the television series *Return to Tuscany*, produced for BBC Television by Seven Stones Media Limited and first broadcast on BBC2 in 2006.

Published by BBC Books, BBC Worldwide Ltd, Woodlands, 80 Wood Lane, London W12 0TT

First published in 2006
Copyright © Seven Stones Media Limited, Giancarlo and Katie Caldesi 2006
The moral rights of the authors have been asserted.

Photographs on pages 5, 23, 27, 30, 35, 46, 47, 53, 57, 66, 67, 69, 73, 76, 77, 87, 91, 95, 98, 108, 113, 117, 125, 131, 135, 136, 147, 151, 153 and 157: Jan Baldwin © BBC Worldwide 2006
Photograph on page 9: © Myles New/Olive Magazine
All other photographs: Jesse Alexander © BBC Worldwide 2006

ISBN 0 563 49354 2

Commissioning editors: Nicky Ross and Stuart Cooper
Project editor: Sarah Reece
Copy editors: Jane Bamforth and Tessa Clark
Designer: Isobel Gillan
Production controller: Kenneth McKay

Set in Myriad
Colour origination by Butler & Tanner Ltd
Printed and bound in Great Britain by CPI Bath

For more information about this and other BBC books, please visit our website on www.bbcshop.com or telephone 08700 777 001.